A Greedy Society

A Greedy Society

Real Estate Mortgage Foreclosures: The Effectiveness and Efficiency of Managing Housing and Financial Issues Not Only for African American Families But Also for All Americans in This Economic Crisis

Charles Henry Orr

Copyright © 2012 by Charles Henry Orr.

ISBN: Softcover   978-1-4691-3853-4
           Ebook   978-1-4691-3854-1

All rights reserved. No part of this book may be reproduced or transmitted in any form or by any means, electronic or mechanical, including photocopying, recording, or by any information storage and retrieval system, without permission in writing from the copyright owner.

This book was printed in the United States of America.

To order additional copies of this book, contact:
Xlibris Corporation
1-888-795-4274
www.Xlibris.com
Orders@Xlibris.com

Dedication

All of my books will be dedicated to my mother, Mattie Lee Orr. I did not get to know my mother for very long because she departed this world at a young age. I was only three years old when she passed away in 1946. She died very young because she became very sick. Mattie and my father, Jim Henry Orr, were struggling to raise four children in Birmingham, Alabama. This was where her struggle ended and ours began. I did not get to know her very well, but she had to be a good person. Losing my mother so soon in life had a profound effect on me. God must have had a very good reason for taking her away so soon. This was why I have always tried to do well in life. I want her to be proud of me. This book is my way of saying, "Thanks, Mattie, for bringing me into this world."

Acknowledgments

This book is written for my brother and my sisters. My sisters are Mrs. Eva Mae Green (Akron, Ohio) and Mrs. Ann Riley (Houston, Texas), and my brother is Art Orr (Chicago, Illinois). This is also for their children and spouses. I want to thank Professor David Anderson, Business Administration and Attorney at Law and Randy Shire, Manager Public Safety Department. Also, thanks to Robert Bradley, Larry Reed, and Seran Woodfort-Bey, my friends and coworkers at DePaul University.

Contents

Chapter 1: Introduction 1
Chapter 2: Review of the Literature 19
Chapter 3: Methodology 33
Chapter 4: Findings 39
Chapter 5: Discussion and Conclusion 45
References 59
Appendices 63
Resume 69

Chapter 1: Introduction

A Greedy Society will show the poor, working, and middle-class people hoping for the American dream being sadly disappointed in America. They have been lied to, cheated, and discriminated against, not only in housing but in employment opportunities as well. This is an investigation of the impact of mortgage foreclosures on African American families and communities in urban areas like Chicago, Illinois. There were one million foreclosures in 2010 in the United States, while Wall Street executives and banks received huge profits from real estate transactions. In this study, the author has covered all aspects of the real estate industry. The main coverage was the problems of foreclosures. The secondary issue in this piece was the African American family's quality of life. How do foreclosure problems affect African Americans' future? Why are African American families and communities more vulnerable? What will the future be like in homeownership for African American families in the United States? These questions were researched and analyzed in this academic book. The subjects of business, sociology, politics, and economics will be used in this discussion. The direct connection to my first book is deliberate. Foreclosures will increase the homeless population and poverty in the United States.

Facing foreclosure is a daunting task for homeowners in the United States. According to Mortgage Bankers Association, one out of every two hundred people will face foreclosure. For example, in a city like Washington DC, three thousand homeowners lose their home each year. Every three months, two hundred fifty thousand new families enter foreclosure. In every classroom in America, there is one child whose parents cannot pay their mortgage. Six of ten homeowners wish they understood more about their mortgage loan documents. More than the same number of homeowners is delinquent on their payments. A slow real estate market causes values and prices to fall. When

1

adjusted rate montages adjust, refinancing is no longer an option as property values decline. Freddie Mac Roper reports (2006),

> A survey of 2,015 people revealed the emotions percentages relative to fear or scarred homeowners. Scared was 38 percent, embracement was 8 percent, depressed people was 35 percent; emotions was 9 percent, and none comprised 9 percent. In the United States of America, families that do not have 3 months savings equal 43 percent and have less than 5,000.00 in the bank. Approximately 43 percent spend more than they earn annually. And 52 percent live paycheck to paycheck. The issues that put families over the edge into foreclosure, 32 percent have lose job, 25 percent have health problems in family, 50 percent have already missed two loan payments, and 85 percent have missed one payment.

Mortgage lenders and investors do not make money on foreclosures; their losses run from 20 to 60 percent of the dollar value of the property. Capitalism traditionally is the economic strategy used in the United States of America. Recent events indicate that this needs some attention by government policy makers. Real estate issues are the centerpiece of the economic downturn we are experiencing today. Lenders of mortgage money such as banks and financial institutions not only contributed to the problems but are also the main players. Subprime loans to unqualified borrowers have led to an unprecedented amount of foreclosures. Foreclosure originates when homeowners do not pay an agreed amount of money toward ownership of their homes. This is in essence the definition of a mortgage loan. Courts act as referees in the foreclosure process. Laws in Illinois are being changed in order to control the ethical behavior of realtors and lenders in the state.

Gambling Away America

This book is relative to the way some people have been trying to live in the last thirty years. Big fancy housing, big fancy trucks and cars, lots of entertainment, and partying seem to be goals for too many Americans. Gambling has become a habit and one of the vehicles for attainment of these things. By gambling, they not only lose money but crash the economy as well. Now it is time to pay back, but no one wants to pay back even if they could. This book is about real estate mortgage foreclosure and greed, which are the most dominating causes of the economic crash. The effects on African American families and communities in cities like Chicago, Illinois, will be highlighted in this book.

In the last six years, homeownership among African Americans has declined at least 60 percent; this is four times more than for white Americans. African Americans can get mostly subprime loans, and white Americans get traditional loans, which means foreclosures are higher in African American neighborhoods. There is a massive increase in renters because of foreclosures. Rental cost has increased as a result. If rent keeps rising, this would put many more people on the streets. If the employment picture does not improve, then the rent will be out of reach as well. Since African Americans are the last to be hired, it would take five to ten years for them to get back into the workforce because of variables such as discrimination, government policies, greed, regulation of policies, ethics, and education.

According to an MSNBC newsperson (June 28, 2010), this foreclosure problem worsens because "the previous presidential administration crashed the economy in the United States by giving Wall Street a free hand." Wall Street, in essence, gambled with our economy. The author thinks that the United States is a reactive society as it relates to money, for example, the real estate bubble, fixing the levees before Katrina happened, and the oil spills on the Gulf Coast by the BP Corporation. He believes greed and the lack of morals influence attitudes of corporation stockholders and elected officials relative to solving problems before they turn into a tragedy. Foreclosures in the United States are a tragedy.

According to *Merriam-Webster Dictionary*, greed is a desire to possess wealth or goods in an unreasonable and/or sinful way. The acts associated with dishonesty, such as cheating, stealing, fraud, and theft, are not ruled out, gambling they will not get caught. Moral deals with and is based on principles such as right and wrong. Behavior also plays an important role relative to morals. Quoting:

> For what is a man profited, if he shall gain the whole world, and lose his own soul? Or what shall a man give in exchange for his soul?
>
> King James Version Holy Bible
> New Testament, Matthew 16:26

This religious quote gives a historical view of the effects of greed relative to humankind. The authors think this was the problem that fueled the economic crisis around the world, and mortgage foreclosures are the result of excessive greed and a lack of moral behavior.

Vantage Points of the Author

In 1979, Orr obtained a sales license in the state of Ohio; he worked as a salesperson for several companies until 1988 in Ohio and Illinois. The first degree earned by Charles was in real estate brokerage in 1981 from the University of Akron. The next year in 1982, he earned another associate degree in business management technology from the same university. 1988 is when he became a broker in Illinois and still is a broker in the Chicago area. This experience qualifies him to focus this book on real estate mortgages and foreclosures. He has owned several houses and has been foreclosed on. From 1983 to 1988 in Chicago, he witnessed the rise of real estate prices because of greed and the loss of morals. These unethical practices led to the situation the United States economy is facing today.

Participatory Observation

In 1983, brokers and mortgage lenders wanted not only to narrow the time period for closing sales but to raise the amounts of money earned on each sale as well. Orr was involved in many real estate transactions and always kept his real estate license in good standing for the last thirty-one years. He stayed up with real estate issues even when not working in the business. Based on not liking the changes in behavior of participants relative to greed, ethics, and lack of morals, Orr decided not work in the industry during the boom of the 1990s. That generation of brokers and lenders clearly wanted to make money as much and as fast as possible, and many did.

The author thinks the real estate industry needs reform and deep regulations not only in the United States but in all societies for three main reasons: shelter, dignity, and assets. Shelter attainment has been challenging for African Americans in the United States. Their dignity has been taken away because of living on the fringes since they were brought here during the slavery years of society. The living condition has not improved very much over the years. Because of lack of assets, they live in the worse-kept areas of the city in most cases. If they buy a home, it is usually in those same communities. These comments are a result of observation by the author. The author has held a real estate broker's license since 1988. He has been involved in more than one hundred real estate transactions in the Chicago area. He has been foreclosed on and lost the home in 1984 because he lost his job in Akron, Ohio. He lost a two-flat building in Chicago, Illinois, by foreclosure; and if it was not for a loan modification, he would have lost his home because of this present crisis. The American dream has always been a primary goal of the author of this book. Homelessness has always been a challenge for African Americans.

A Brief Case Study

Charles H. Orr Real Estate Company relates to foreclosures not only of the company office but also of residents. In 1977, he brought his first house in Akron, Ohio. This was a two-story, three-bedroom framed dwelling with an enclosed front porch; this is where the office began in 1979 when Orr became an agent in the state of Ohio. There was a serious fire in this house, and it was totally by an insurance company that no one was hurt. He purchased another house instead of repairing that one. The real estate office was in the basement in this house. In 1981, he graduated with a real estate brokerage degree but did not get a brokerage license in Ohio until 1993. However, he acquired a brokerage license in Illinois in 1988.

The first house was foreclosed on for back taxes some years later, or I should say a lot. The second home was lost to foreclosure because of a marriage separation that ended in divorce in 1984. Orr continued working as an agent in Illinois from 1983 until he started his own business in 1988. As an agent for another company, he was personally involved in over one hundred real estate transactions in the Chicago area. He purchased a two-flat building for rental income in 1987 but lost it to foreclosure in 1991 after the tenants trashed it and the insurance company would not cover the damages. Orr kept his real estate active all during the 1990's real estate boom. He kept thinking about reentering the business but was forced to work in another area. He had an office in his apartment, but with trying to make a living, he completely missed out on the large sums of profits many real estate agents and brokers received during that time. After he saw the way they were acting relative to greed and fraud during that time, he is glad he did not get involved.

In all of the years since 1990, he has taken and passed the two-year requirement of continuing education for real estate brokers in Illinois. He has also gone back to college and acquired his bachelor's degree, his master's in sociology, and a doctorate in business administration, all but a dissertation. He missed out on the money for knowledge. The latter was the best decision because he has been able to retain a home that he purchased in 2004, and it was foreclosed on in 2008, but he got it back through a loan modification, and he still has a home real estate office with computer technology in his control. Orr plans to continue writing books and selling real estate in spring of 2012.

The lesson here is twofold: never give up on your dreams and never stop trying. Orr was fighting to stay employed and to keep a roof over his head all his life. This story was told to show how hard it is for African Americans to acquire the things they need to live decently in the United States. The economic crisis we are experiencing today will be so hard on African Americans it just might cause it to be a homeless race in America. This will happen if the people do not stop the division of the races, and all of us must work hard and together to prevent such a tragedy in this democratic society.

A Story of How and Why Orr Purchased His Present Home

Charles Orr purchased a three-bedroom raised ranch brick home on the south side of Chicago in 2004. This is a single-family house with a two-car detached garage. The home was built in 1964. There is one identical home on each side of it except Orr's has three bedrooms. These other two homes have only two bedrooms each. They all were built at the same time. Orr's house was a bank-reposed property at the time of purchase and was priced at $106,000. He paid $102,000 and got a $3,000 from the seller for repairs. The mortgage was a conventional one with 7.25 percent interest rate.

The down payment was supposed to have been 10 percent, but with credits and prorations, he paid only $3,000 at the closing and used $7,000 to make some repairs, which included painting and replacing fixtures such as doors, windows, and locks. Orr had good credit and a down payment but had a low-paying job. He had been saving for the nine years he lived in the same apartment. He needed a home; it is fair to say this is the first real home he has had in sixty-seven years on this earth. The American dream has always been hard to obtain for African Americans in this society. Chicago can change according to the block you are living in. His block is basically quiet because older people live there for years. The lady next door to Orr was an original owner when these units were built in 1964.

Orr thinks these are some smart steps to buying a bank-reposed house or an HUD house that has been vacant for a while and what to look for at the beginning.

1. You need a job with at least two years of service and have saved up a down payment that has been in the bank for at least six months before attempting to purchase your new home.

2. Get a credit report and clean up any debt problems so it shows payment of bills on time for at least twelve consecutive months.
3. Find a bank or mortgage company in good standing to qualify you for a loan. In today's market, FHA (Federal Housing Authority) has the best loan-qualifying programs for anyone that really wants to purchase a home.
4. Once the largest amount you can afford to pay for a home is determined, find a broker to show you homes for sale.
5. Don't pay that much if possible and use saving for repairs if the home needs extensive repairs but is in the area or neighborhood. FHA can build these repairs into the loan payments with a program called 203b.
6. Contact a real estate broker to show you homes in your price range.
7. Again, make sure the broker is honest and in good standing in the industry. Deal with the one you believe you can trust and is interested not only in their commission but in fairness to your interest as well.
8. If the home needs repairs, make sure the work is still within your total price range.
9. Have a home inspector and contractor give opinion before closing the sale.
10. Put this in your contract that it is contingent on inspector and contractor reports, if possible.

These steps could lead to a successful purchase without any unethical practice being involved.

Figure 1.

The following poem was written by Orr (2001)

> It takes more than a notion
> To be a real estate broker.
> It takes more than a token
> To keep the office open.
>
> Working hard with prospects,
> Closing many deals.
> Keep them from being suspects,
> So you won't be spending your wheels.

It takes plenty of skills,
People skills at its best
Knowledge that spills;
So you don't make a mess:
Of the best real estate deals.

Market analysis and information,
Can bring you plenty of joy.
When you use integrity,
Like a child uses a toy.

Real estate is a numbers game,
Giving benefits and taking names.
By helping families find a home,
Then you haven't done any wrong.

It is easy to get greedy,
Thinking of your wants instead of the needy.
It is hard to make money,
It is easy when you don't get funny.

It takes ambitions and persistence
To get plenty of assistance.
Selling real estate is a chore
It is not a job for a bore.

Character and discipline is real,
When you are trying to make a deal.
Being straight keeps you strong;
So you won't do any wrong.

Figure 2.

Flowchart

Chapter 1: Introduction
Chapter 2: Review of the Literature
Chapter 3: Methodology
Chapter 4: Findings
Chapter 5: Discussion and Conclusion
References
Appendices

This is the order in which events will occur in this piece.

Definitions

- African Americans are 12 percent of the population of approximately 330 million people. Their ancestors came mostly from west or central African and were slaves. There are some thirty million African Americans living in America today. The author may refer to them as black people in this book.
- Real estate is land and improvement such as buildings, fences, wells, and fixtures that are nor immovable. It includes property in buildings and land and anything permanent attached to the land. The effects of real estate values on the economy will be investigated in this book.
- Mortgage and foreclosure: A mortgage is the transfer of property used as security of payment of a debt, while foreclosure is the legal procedure of foreclosing a mortgage.
- Homeless race is created by this author to show concern about the rapid multiplications of homeless veterans and others living on American streets and how the numbers are increasing so fast. This is very scary especially during this economic crisis.

- Ethics is a discipline that deals with good and evil and with moral duty.
- Moral and attitude: morals deal with right and wrong, and attitude refers to behavior of the mind. The author used these key words to highlight the discussions in this book.
- Gambling is the wagering of money or something of material value.
- Regulation is detailed orders issued by an executive authority of a government and having the force of law.
- Greed is attitudes of selfish desire beyond reason such as Wall Street executives selling the economy for personal gain.
- Irresponsibility refers to the federal government's lack of intervention to the actions on Wall Street's greedy efforts.

Statement of the Problem

There has been a paradigm shift in the area of business, economics, ethics, and financial policies, not only in the United States, but in the rest of the world as well. Multinational Corporation is one of the main players of the economic crisis. The generation of children born in the 1970s came of age in the 1990s. They are in their forties now and in many cases are running things they rebelled against the norms established by past generations. This was the beginning of a shift in behavior in the United States. Many of this generation became addicted to gambling, drugs, and sex, which many elected officials encouraged in the name of increased revenue to boost the economy. The gambling has expanded around the country because it was not convenient to go to Los Vegas all the time. The drug abuse started a war on smoking cigarettes and was replaced by marijuana that led to cocaine and stronger drugs. The sex issue came out in the open because this generation decided not to be ashamed and wanted to have sex with anyone they wish, whether a man or woman of the same sex. Today, they are getting married to the same sex. It is amazing how this behavior has changed in America since 1970.

This author thinks this it is connected to foreclosure problems because all of these habits involve spending money. Gaming, drugs, and sex can be very expensive habits. Gambling away bill and mortgage money is not uncommon today. Drugs abusers not only use all their money but tend to steal from relatives or anyone else to pay for drugs. Sex gets expensive when married people with children maintain outside affairs, whether with the opposite-sex or the same-sex partner. Some people engage in all three of these activities. If they have a mortgage, keeping up would be hard regardless of income amounts.

Gentrification is when more affluent people influenced by government policies take depressed communities and forced the poor out by moving in and changing the tax base. Sadly, the author thinks that cities like Chicago, with high immigrations rates, may leave the poor on the south and west side homeless. There are millions of homeowners on the fringes of foreclosure because they paid too much for their homes in the first place, and the cost of money (interest) is too high, or the cost of the house is too high, which is still to the lender's advantage. According to the National Mortgage News (2006), subprime funders originated 809 billion in home mortgages in 2005, a 28 percent increase from the year before. These were newly released figures from the *Quarterly Data Report* (QDR), which is published by the National Mortgage News. The top three companies are Countrywide, Wells Fargo, and Washington Mutual. Lenders of all stripes originated 3.29 trillion in home loans in 2005. This was the industry's second best year ever.

Real estate issues are the main focus in this study. The problem is that the foreclosure rates in poverty areas are very high, and investors are going into these areas and buying up property at low prices and building expensive condos or new homes that will be marketed to a different group of people. Investors buy with cash and repair or rebuild the property through refinancing, which involves a mortgage in most cases. The displacement of the original group living in these areas brings up the question: are they being treated fairly in light of their economic position? The author thinks that with inflated real estate prices for houses, mortgage loan companies should consider that people of modest income may fall behind a month or two and should not be so quick to threaten them with foreclosure procedures. Government intervention and reform are dispersedly needed in this area.

Purpose of Study

The purpose of this research is for people to be aware that African American families have had problems finding suitable living accommodations in the United States. They were denied mortgages for years. In the boom period of the 1990s, lenders started giving them loans out of greed for profits. They knew these people could not keep these properties but forgot their morals for plain old greed. Deregulation by the government for banks and lending institutions in the 2000 drove this industry insane with greed. The author hopes the real estate industry will be regulated again, and discrimination practices toward blacks and minorities be stopped in relation to housing in this society. The economy cannot stand more of these immoral business practices of a few that not only will affect the United States economy but the world economy as well. This study came about because the real estate bubble has busted, and greed and lack of morals are part of the basic cause of this dilemma. The author wishes to add to the research on foreclosures.

Managing financial situations is a problem for not only many African Americans but for many other human beings around the world as well. The main reason is not only education but the lack of access to money also. Supervising money matter is referred to as financial literacy in most cases today. Many educators argue this should be taught in early childhood in schools around the world instead of waiting until bad habits as consumers have set in too deep. Counseling at this point in most cases will be useless to many. Teaching financial literacy to adults with formal education is hard and almost impossible for those without any previous education. Based on personal observation by the author, there are some successful money managers that do not have much education.

African Americans homeowners are losing in financial crisis. They lead in foreclosures in the United States. The only team players are family, and in most cases, none of them have enough income to help in times like these. Eighty percent of families in the country are single parent households, and women are running things in most families in African American communities. The males either are not there or are not employed or underemployed. If family members cannot contribute to the household expenses, then the possibility of foreclosure increases tragically. All family members need to learn and be more organized, and learn more about financial literacy, and try harder to curve spending unnecessarily. They should stay together and care more about one another and focus on having a better future for themselves and their family. The author thinks much of this can be accomplished through education.

Managing one's self relative to ethical behavior can be very difficult in the business world. There are several factors that affect ethical behavior. If they are employees of a company, corporation, or other types of organization, whose policies are ethically questionable, then following these policies can lead to unethical acts that as an individual they would not participate. Codes of ethics by some organizations are not very good, or no one follows them. There are internal and external stakeholders in organizations. The law relative to ethics can overlap and become an ethical dilemma. Organizational structure and culture play a major role in its ethical practices.

Many corporations have rules in place regarding ethics; however, the culture of the organizations determines compliance based on the degree they increase profit margins. Motivation factors in the real estate industry can be huge for multinational corporations because the author thinks investors and foreign interest in the real estate market in the United States is very high, because they want to live here. Policy of government officials allow not only investment but supervise immigration to the United States as well. Hopefully, under the new administration, leadership can curve some of this activity. Legal counsel may determine these things to be legal, but the question remains: is it ethical? This economic crisis should teach that greed on the part of a few can affect all. Learning lessons from this will not only take time but some attitude changes as well. It will require character to learn what need to know about managing life. African Americans need to try harder in financial issues. They need to stay focus on their future in this country. And they need to care more for themselves, their children, and others as well

Banks and mortgage loan companies freed up their lending practices, and many consumers refinanced their home, and others purchased homes they could not afford. As a result, managing these situations became daunting, if not impossible, tasks that have produced an epidemic called foreclosures in the United States. The homeless population was already at record heights; now they are phenomenal in proportions. The motivation to own their own home is very high, but most lack the ability to act on them. The failure to supervise their funds well is just one reason for the inability of African Americans to buy and keep their homes. Even for the ones with the funds, financial counseling is needed in most cases to keep it.

According to Castaneda's (2004) dissertation, titled "Financial Literacy," teaching financial literacy in African American families and communities is critically needed so they can manage money and keep their homes. Learning when the race has been deprived of knowledge for so long will be a real challenge for many of them. They need to try harder to handle financial matters better. Staying on what is perceived as a low-paying job can pay off in the long run. The author started in a low-paying occupation fourteen years ago; he managed to make a good living by working overtime. There was plenty because the turnover rate in that occupation was very high. He understood the problem of being unemployed and cared enough about himself to tough it out, while others would just quit. Rohm (1993) said, "Keep trying until your skills change."

Financial literacy is necessary, not only for African Americans but also for all Americans, so they can learn how to handle money matters better. Trying to save money in a capitalist economy is not easy for anyone; however, this is the key to being financial literate. Teaching and learning about financial matters will help the entire economy be better off. Staying in school for all children is critical in today's world. People in America do not care enough about their living expenses; rather, people too often put other things like cars and entertainment before living expenses.

President Barack Obama said in the State of Union address in 2010: "The best solution for poverty is a world-class education." The author thinks families get in financial trouble when they do not work like a team in the home.

Humankind's greed contributed to the economic crisis and the real estate foreclosure problems, not only in the United States but around the world as well. In the 1980s, the lights in major cities was turned down to save energy and to reduce activities of the people after dark. This left the American population in the darkness at least three generations. Race, greed, and wealth are variables in this darkness in America. The real estate industry was the centerpiece on much of this greed. Many brokers and lenders got rich during the boom of the 1990s. African Americans and other minorities were used to fuel these unethical business practices such as subprime mortgage issues and fraudulent lending. *A Homeless Race* will show the poor working and middle class hoping for the American dream will have many serious challenges in the future.

This is an investigation of the impact of mortgage foreclosures on African American families in urban areas like Chicago, Illinois. The *Chicago Sun Times* (2009) article predicts foreclosures will continue to be a problem in 2012 and perhaps even longer because of high unemployment rates. Since 2005, foreclosure filings in this area have reached 192,460, according to this article. African American neighborhoods are hit the hardest. The south and west sides of Chicago will be changed relative to demographics in the future. Investors and speculators don't care about these areas and the problems for these people; they hope they can sell for a profit in two or three years. There have been 66,930 in the city alone since 2005. 2008 was the worse year not only for Illinois but for the rest of the country as well. The quality of life of African American people has been seriously affected by the foreclosure problems in America.

The Fair Housing Act in the United States indicates no discrimination on the basis of race, sex, religion, color, familiar status, national origin, and handicapped human beings (according to Connerly 2006). The author thinks that these are good laws, but many do not always adhere to these laws. The connection to mortgage foreclosures and African American families is that if you are black, you are likely to be discriminated against in any of these areas in America. He will admit without these laws in place, the situation would be considerably worse. For example, African Americans pay taxes and insurance for their property just like everyone else; nevertheless, insurance companies are less likely to pay damages in poor communities.

In recent years, many homeowners refinanced their homes, drawing down large sums in the form of equity. In many cases, they inflated the prices and were giving people money equaling over 100 percent equity, with adjustable mortgages. The poor money management practices not only of the mortgage lenders but on the part of many homeowners as well led to the massive amounts of forecloses we see today in the United States. The author thinks greed is the motivating factor on the part of all stakeholders. The lack of supervision and/or regulation assisted this mess as well. Counsel was given by some economic experts, but no one was listening. The bubble has burst, and not only is this country hurting but others also. The housing market is the key element in this financial crisis.

The American Recovery and Reinvestment Act of 2009 gave greatly needed funding to several organizations for aid for the hungry and homeless families in the United States. According to the US Conference of Mayor's Report for 2010, there is an increase in homeless families in 2010. This report is not absolute, but it is also creditable as a guide to understating the homeless problem in the United States. This author thinks the increase in homeless families has a direct relationship to the foreclosure problems. The city of Chicago was one of the cities in this report and received funding from the Recovery and Reinvestment Act.

The strategies used in business settings should be used in the home as well. There has to be a leader at home. Women tend to have this job in African American families. They need to go back to college to learn financial literacy. Wall Street executives are making huge bonuses, while maim street suffers. Corporations and shareholders have shown their morals are not functioning properly. What they fail to realize is that their actions affect all stakeholders, meaning the rest of society. The real estate market was hit by a paradigm shift when subprime lenders gave loans over the actual value of the property. Managers of these lenders saw investors outside of the United States would pay huge prices for property in the this country.

Lipman (2008), Immergluck (2008), and Howell (2006) seemed to recognize the reasons for so many homeowners having foreclosure problems in the study that follows. According to Lipman's (2008) study, titled "Mixed-Income Schools and Housing Advancing the Neoliberal Urban Agenda," Chicago, Denver, and Philadelphia are only three cities in America where mixed-income schools are being used. Quoting Dr. Lipman from the University of Chicago:

> What would count as education policy if it would include strategies to increase minimum wage, investing in urban job creation and training, provide funds for college completion to those who cannot afford it, and enforce laws that would end racial segregation in housing and hiring? (13)

The primary issue includes neoliberalism, race, and housing in order to show that the social justice and/or fair treatment among the people would be good for all stakeholders. This article was written to highlight mixed-income schools and social justice on behalf of black and minority groups living in poverty in the United States. The secondary issue includes mixed-income schools, social justice, and poverty. The strength was that Lipman (2008) argues that the systems of cities like Chicago and other cities would not help the poverty and segregation problems in the long run. There were no obvious weaknesses in these studies, and they were well written and organized, which fit my study very well. It gives me the opportunity to see how housing and education can change people's life.

Maslow's hierarchy of needs theory was based in psychology and deals with human motivation. These needs included psychological, safety, love and belonging, esteem, and self-actualization. The ownership of homes for humans fulfills many of these needs (1943). McGregor's XY theories (1960) involves the trust that people can be trusted to do their jobs well or not. Theory X do not get as good results as theory Y, which gives people more trust than X does. These theories fit my topic because of the ethics of financial institutions, and Wall Street has behaved in this crisis we are trying to recover from now. Greed and morals are connected to psychology and motivation.

The character of men and women are being questioned around the world today. Adam Smith discussed ethics in business, which has a direct relationship to dishonesty and character. He referred to the invisible hand influencing business, and it still does today; only the hands are not invisible today. Business ethics has broken down and dissolved in today's world of work. Many misguided executives and employees will bypass dignity for a profit. Good and evil are seen daily in every area of business. Good people turn bad because of greed and the concepts of making more money. Corporations become God to many people because they control much of the wealth in the world. Economies are destroyed because of the lack of morals and greed.

Real estate and business issues at the beginning of this century have experienced a paradigm shift based on financial activity around the world. Fraud has moved in on much of the business scene and disrupted the day-to-day activity of many businesses. This is especially visible in the real estate industry by the number of foreclosures reported. Mortgage lending dominated the industry with refinancing existing loans and selling them to investors around the world. Wall Street executives made billions of dollars selling financial instruments and stocks relative to the real estate industry in the United States. Shareholders and stakeholders also gained huge profits because of this paradigm shift. Many profited from the boom now that the bubble has busted and it is payback time, which is causing many problems around the world.

According to Immergluck (2008), subprime mortgages from 1997 to 2003, there were high levels of subprime mortgages in 103 metropolitan areas with 500,000 populations or more. Many of these areas were African American communities. Investors came into these areas and made cheap purchases in some cases and sold properties to poor people with a subprime mortgage, who would eventually go into foreclosure because they could afford these homes in the first place. The role of the Department of Housing and Urban Development (HUD) in foreclosures is managing these homes until someone, who is usually an investor, bids on them. They would repair the home as cheap as possible and sell it to some poor soul that wanted a home desperately. The rich people on Wall Street sold bad paper to other rich people buying stocks at risk that they knew would go badly at the expense of the rest of us.

When the financial system crashed they wanted us to bail them out, and we had to do that or have a situation similar to the Great Depression of the 1930s. This is what the people at Goldman Sachs were basically doing when we bailed them out. When real estate is sold, the buyer purchases two things: the property and the money or mortgage; the cost of money is the interest. If the buyer missed enough payment, the lender opts for a foreclosure, but the buyer can redeem if the values and prices can be obtained. The income of the borrower plays a major role in the mortgage process. Rental perpetrates is going better since the problems of foreclosures have exploded.

According to this quote, "Managers are people who do things right, and leaders are people who do the right thing," Warren Bennis argues that leaders' decisions are more important than managers' decisions. The author agrees with this argument because ethics and morals are major variables in decision making. Ethics involve knowing right from wrong, and morals involve fair play from a religious perspective. Managers tend to focus on getting the task done as effective as possible; whether that is ethical and/or moral does not enter into this decision as much as it could. The decisions made in our current real estate foreclosure problems seem not to consider ethics or morals, just making profits for a small number of corporations, executives, and individuals.

Chapter 2: Review of the Literature

A homeless culture has been created in the United States. Not only African American males but women and children are homeless and living on the streets as well. Statistics show that the highest of the homeless population today are children under nine years old. The parents that have a job don't earn enough to maintain shelter. People are homeless when they live with relatives or friends after age eighteen in the United States. More people are staying at home until they can afford a house or apartment. In a city like Chicago, a single person needs to make $17.00 per hour for forty hours a week because it is hard to find a decent place to live under $1,000.00 per month. Most African Americans do not make close to this amount. If two of them get a place together, they are still statistically homeless because without their partner, they could not live there.

Financial and Economic Issues

Shlay's (2006) article, titled "Low-Income Homeownership: American Dream or Delusion," hit the heart of why the author wrote this book. The primary issue includes policies dealing with low-income home ownership and all of the variables related to it. The secondary issue was the way this argument diverted the policy maker's obligation to create policies for affordable housing. This piece was written to amplify how law makers in the United States avoid issues affecting the low-income or poor minority of the population in the United States of America. The setting was in any city or small town where the poor are in need of affordable housing. The regulatory policies in the housing industry were not to build affordable housing; rather, the policy was to sell high-priced houses to low-income people.

The author's thoughts center around greed and immoral practices on the part of real estate brokers, lending institutions, and government policies. This article was strong in explaining the reasons why the American dream is a delusion in America. The only weakness the above groups mentioned was not giving the correct verdict because getting people to buy homes they could not afford lies in the real estate broker's part, getting people to refinance with adjustable rate mortgages on the part of the lenders, and the government not having policies and regulations in place to prevent all of this from happening. Campaign contributions on the part of public officials were where greed can play into as well. The opportunity here is for the policies and regulations to be changed in the future. Shlay (2006) also argues that "the elevation of low-income homeownership to its present status was to deflect political attention away from alternative policies for affordable housing." A threat based on this article was that she argues that the concept of the American dream was introduced by the political right, and that this is and always has been a delusion on the part of Americans. The author agrees not only with this argument, but African Americans and other minorities in particular.

According to Bond and Williams's (2007) article, "Residential Segregation and the Transformation of Home Mortgage Lending," the primary issue was to show that the lending to low-income and minority buyers starting in the 1990 did not affect separation in cities like Chicago. The secondary issue was deregulation of the mortgage lending industry transformed that business from redlining practicing of the past. Redlining means not lending to black or African American borrowers. The article was written to demonstrate this move in lending did not help the segregation of different groups in America. After decades of residential segregation and redlining, lending institutions started giving mortgages to black and minority borrowers throughout the United States. The objective was to influence the real estate sales and profit margins. The data came from Home Owners Disclosure Act 1992 to 1999 and the 1990 to 2000 Census Data.

The strength of this research was the discovery of the underlining reason why all of a sudden loans are provided to blacks and minority groups. The author thinks this was motivated by greed. The weakness seems to have been not telling the readers enough about how redlining and separating human beings in any society is divisible and not in the best interest of that society. The opportunity Bond and Williams (2007) had was to show how African Americans are a homeless race and has been denied and displaced in housing issues since the years of slavery in the United States. The author of this piece thinks a threat to the issues of segregation and mortgage lending is too late because African Americans are living in poverty situations, living with parents and grandparents, living with friends, living on the streets, or that a combination of all of these has been going on for years. The future does not show any changes in these issues, and it seems they may increase. If they cannot pay for an apartment with their income, they are homeless in the view of the author.

According to Bertrand, Mullainathan, and Shafir (2006), "Behavior economics and marketing in aid of decision making among the poor," The primary issue was psychological perspective in decision making not only by the poor but for others as well. The reason this article was written was to demonstrate how the lack of monetary resources affects decision making by the poor. The issues that matter relative to implications for future policies are as follows:

- Simplicity for filling out forms and applying for benefits offered by government policy.
- Persuasion relative to poor people's participation in programs that would help them.
- Marketing government and nonprofits are rare; perhaps, they should do more of this type of informing people.
- Program details could be better understood if marketed correctly.
- Honesty and accountability are very important in communicating to the poor by government agencies.

The behavior of the poor affects their decision-making abilities because of trials and tribulations, and living day to day on the fringes of the larger society puts undue stress on the brain. The ability to think is affected. Some strengths of this study is to let society know that the poor needs help. It lets them know that the consequences of not helping the poor can be in the form of violence and other undesirable social problems like criminal activities such as arson, which cost the rest of society in many ways. The weaknesses of this study were few, but there are many tools for improving the thinking of humans such as education. The opportunity here would be financial literacy classes for the poor supported by the government though nonprofit organizations. A threat relative to foreclosures and other real estate issues is there will be more homeless people on the streets. Employment and education for the poor in this society should be at the top of the agenda for leaders and elected officials in the United States. The author thinks greed and the lack of morals have contributed to the growing numbers of poor people in this society.

According to Clark's (2009) argument in his article, titled "A Christian

Perspective of the Current Economic Crisis," is the primary issue of the current economic crisis that was based on unbalanced lives where the economy was built on social injustice and greed. The reason this article was written from a Christian perspective was that the problems in this world has a direct relationship with human's relationship with a belief in a higher power (i.e., God). The secondary issue looks at income disparity and or inequality not only in the United States but the in rest of the world as well.

The strength of this research was centered in Christianity though and the principles involved relative to beliefs in God's rules for living in this world. For example, we should "do unto others as we want them to do with us." The weaknesses of this study could be selling religious thought in economics will be a hard sell in a world where greed and a lack of morals are almost the norm. There is an opportunity here by creating a "just economy," which is what is needed not only in the United States but also throughout the world. A threat in this research could be using principle instead of methodology and theories used in scientific research.

Orr thinks the connection to our foreclosure problems in the African American communities is very apparent in this article. African Americans as a whole believe in God; this may be why they have survived all this time. They are becoming a homeless race because the unbalanced income and unbalanced economy referred to by Clark (2009). A "just economy" should be the goal.

Barolo and Hochguertel (2007) argue in "Household Debt and Credit: Economic Issues and Data Causes of Problems" that there is not enough data on UN household liabilities in many countries, and that there is a need to look at consumer debt around the world. The primary issue was household debt including mortgages credit problems as well. The secondary issue was to make sure the data are correct and abundant throughout the world. The strength lies in the time of publishing in 2007 because of the bubble burst in 2008.

Financial reform has taken place in the United States and in other countries as well. The authors were on time in writing this piece. One weakness was worrying about data collection too much; it is now known that the available data were correct. An opportunity for these researchers was they can stay ahead in their analysis of household debt and the data acknowledgement of the information. No threats are recognized by this author, but he thinks the article connects to his research because debt and credit are the centerpiece of real estate foreclosure problems.

Regulation Issues Relative to Real Estate Sales and Mortgage Lending

According to Connerly's (2006) outline of the "Fair Housing in the US and UK," discrimination practices and other problems in housing are monitored by the Department of Housing and Urban Development (HUD) in the United States. This piece compared fair housing laws in the United States and the United Kingdom with housing discrimination. The secondary issue illustrates their differences and what each can learn from these differences in fair housing laws.

This study was very strong in 2006. The strength lies in the attention it gives to human rights. However, things have changed since that time not only in the United States and the United Kingdom, but in the rest of the world as well. The election of President Barack Obama in the United States in. 2008 has put all areas of discrimination on the table for all to see. Quoting Obama, "Discrimination against African Americans or black people is a good example of man's inhumanity to man in the world."

One weakness in this article asks the following question: why does discrimination against blacks and minority groups in housing cause so much harm to the survival and quality of life of these groups in America? The point is that white people are very uncomfortable integrating with black and minority groups, perhaps because of the way they treated them in the past. Slavery is a good example. There is no need for an examination of slavery and Jim Crow at this time.

An opportunity is that discrimination in housing could be helpful in bringing people together in the future by talking about it more. In 2010, people are not only talking about it but are also acting out in some shameful ways such as using abusive language and spitting on black politicians in the United States. Some possible threats could be violent retaliation by blacks or minority groups. Passing policies will set the civil rights act back and cause all types of other problems. This author thinks that President Obama's agenda for America could help, but are the American people ready to stop discriminating against each other?

Edmiston (2009) tells us about "Characteristics of High-Foreclosure Neighborhoods in the Tenth District." The primary issue of this analysis was low-income foreclosure rates where the crisis started because of subprime mortgages in these areas. The secondary issue was to show how over time the foreclosure crisis moved into higher-income areas between 2006 and 2009 and some reasons for this happening. The locations in this analysis were Wyoming, Colorado, Nebraska, and Florida.

The purpose for writing of the study was that there are considerable variations across geographical areas. The strength of this analysis reveals that the foreclosure crises affect all homeowners in varied degrees throughout the United States. This tells us that the current unemployment rarest not only of low-income workers but of high income workers as well could have been a tragedy without the stimulus package by the federal government in 2009. The weakness of this analysis could be not giving enough attention to the gambling taking place on Wall Street relative to home mortgages. The author passes up an opportunity to discuss policy reform that is needed across the board in the real estate industry in the United States. The obvious threat could be foreclosure worsens and the country falls deeper into recession. This author thinks this was an excellent analysis of the foreclosure crisis.

According to Fuentes's (2009) article titled "Defaulting the American Dream: Predatory Lending in Latino Communities Reform of California's Lending Laws," the primary issue was the impact that predatory lending has played on poor and low-income people seeking the American dream. The purpose for writing this piece seems to be an attempt to get states like California to reform its lending laws relative to predatory and fraudulent practice in real estate sales and mortgage lending. The secondary issue focuses on greed and the lack of morals relative to people who cannot help themselves and who are too trusting in real estate matters.

From 2005 to 2009, even today, the laws are not set to protect poor and minority potential homebuyers not only in California but in the rest of this country as well. The strength was the awareness of how bold and widespread predatory lending is and the strong role they played in this economic downturn. A weakness was the author should have recognized that just because the buyer could not speak English, he has caused the problems because he should not have bought this house knowing he could not pay the cost each month. The opportunity of using better stories to illustrate points about predatory lending, a real threat to the American dream in this authors mind, lies in jealousy among human beings. Greed among the affluent and the lack of morals among the masses contribute greatly to the lack of laws against fraud and predatory.

Statman's (2009) article, "Regulating Financial Markets: Protecting Us from Ourselves and Others," tried to find a balance between free trade and regulated markets. The secondary issue observed humans behavior toward one another relative to free trade. Discovering they will not treat each other fair means stronger regulation would protect us against ourselves and other people. It will force most of us to deal more fairly in business and financial matters. This article was written to show the free market believers that not only can one institution bring down others, but financial markets are built on confidence and trust as well. The strengths of this piece are many, but the discussion on the causes and effects of the financial crisis in the United States stood out here. He was very strong inn his analysis of this financial crisis that affected the world because Wall Street investors gambled with the economy. Weaknesses in this article were few, because everything about who, when, what, where, why, and how was discussed in this article. This crisis provides us with the opportunity to pay back for living above our means into the past and make changes to protect us in the future. The threat would be if critics of stronger financial regulations should block any attempts made by the federal government in this regard. This author thinks (Statman 2009) that the article relates to all the issues in this book.

According to Landis and Mc Cluire (2010), "Rethinking Federal Housing Policy," there were three issue concerning housing investigated in this study: affordable housing, assist low-income renters, and enforced fair housing act in the United States. This article was written to evaluate and analyze trends in housing policies and organization administrating these policies in order to make them more effective. The method used was to revise the history of housing policies and programs to ascertain the effectiveness of these programs. They look at empirical studies as well. The results relative to recommendations were focused on low- and moderate-income families and provide the funding to keep proven programs growing and make them easier to access and more transparent.

The strengths of this study centered on helping the poor acquire affordable housing with the help of government intervention by improving housing policies in the United States.

Weaknesses of this article were few based on its goals. The opportunity of this piece could be that government officials and policy makers use some of these recommendations in future policy.

The threat here will be relative to the attitude of people who are critical in helping blacks and minority groups obtain a better quality of life though housing policy changes. This author reflects on the problems his family has endured by not being able to afford adequate housing because of unfair housing policies and practices. The African American families suffer the most frustration in this area because of discrimination and even today struggle the most with homelessness in America.

Holtoke (2004) tells us about "Community Mobilization and Credit: The Impact of Nonprofits and Social Capital on Community Reinvestment Act Lending" and the reason for writing it. This was focused in the Washington DC area investigating policies that require partnership will the federal and local governments and nonprofit community organization and social capital of individuals to solve the social problems of that community. The author's findings indicate this may work in some areas but not in areas such as those of poor African American communities. The primary issue in this article was to get problems solved by people in that community so the federal government could limit and reduce the assistance provided. The secondary issue was to push communities to take action on their own problems. This does not work in areas where poverty rates are high, because policies require them to act for their own interest. This author thinks this is why the problems in these areas are so bad.

The strength of this study was that the author discovered that this bottom-up approach in solving social problems in communities could not be sustainable without serious financial help from federal and local government. A weakness was this approach has led to many deteriorating communities not only in places like Washington DC but in the rest of this country as well. The opportunity that was lost could have benefited the rebuilding of the United States.

The threat today is that government policy makers keep procrastinating on the revitalization of America. Also, this study was done in 2004, when economic foreclosure posed big problems; it could be many years before this country gets redeveloped.

Ethics in Life and Business

According to Mazer and Ariely's (2006) study, "Dishonesty in Everyday Life and Its Policy Implications," focusing on large corporations such as Enron, Tyco, WorldCom, and others, dishonesty in day-to-day life is so high among too many of us. The primary issue and the secondary issue in this study are greed and morals. Greed and morals are not only the secondary issue in this study but in this author's research as well as he writes about foreclosures in America and the impact it is having on African American families

The strengths include looking at dishonest behavior in several ways: caused by external rewards, internal reward mechanism and caused by self-deception. From a psychological perspective, the authors use internal issues to change or prevent dishonest behavior in life.

The weaknesses involve morality, ethics, and greed. All three of these could be characterized as internal feelings leading toward behavior problems in human beings. The opportunity for future research is at hand because of the way people can change their behavior and their minds. The only real threat is they change their behavior in a negative direction. Anyone paying attention in today's world can see many young people going in the wrong direction, but hopefully that will pass by in the future, and they will start back going the right direction. For example, young African American males with their pants hanging down, they could end up taking them off, and they could pull them up and be men again. This author thinks that eventually they will stop acting like boys and/or girls, and be men again. In life, everything is connected, so internal behavior and external behavior affect progress in life. Losing or not even having a home stops and slows progress in life.

According to Bowman and Williams (1997), "Ethics in Government: From a Winter of Dispirit to a Spring of Hope," improving the leadership of public service in America is emphasized. The American Society of Public Administrations (ASPA) assisted in this study. The primary issues were ethics in society, integrity, and moral standards in organizational conduct. The secondary issues involve codes of ethics, and the American Society of Public Administration gave a survey to 750 of its members in 1996. The foundation for these data that produced a code of ethics for government and political conduct was created. The setting was the political arena looking at public service and public management relative to ethical behavior.

This was one of the strengths found in this piece. Since 1996, the conduct of politics and public officials has taken its toll not only in the United States but around the world as well.

The weakness could be that in 2010, fourteen years later, the code of ethics in many organizations does not prevent bad behavior and dishonesty on the part of its members. An opportunity could come from the hope for reform proposed by President Obama's administration. The threat is there will not be any reform in government policies because of opposition in Congress. The United States continue down a path of greed and lack of morals.

I think the study hit the heart of what is wrong in America from top to bottom. The ones with wealth are tiring to increase it; the ones without wealth are doing anything to get it. This is what happens during the real estate boom of the 1990s. People seem to be so obsessed that they don't care if they lose their home in foreclosure; this is demonstrated by increased gambling in America. Even Wall Street became a gambling boat for the wealthy investors.

According to Wight's (2007) article, "The Treatment of Smith's Invisible Hand, How Human Nature Direct Behavior which Is the Primary Issue," this invisible hand operates in many institutional settings and affects economic progress. This method by Smith connects to our economic crisis by pronominal acts of greed not only on Wall Street but in many other areas as well. Wall Street executives packaged subprime mortgages and sold them around the world, knowing they were too risky for investors and would not be sustainable over time.

This was strong and well written relative to human behavior that affects their morals and ethical activities. Wealth is not the only thing affecting happiness, according to Adam Smith.

Self-interest is an instinct for human beings. Morals and the notion of good and evil are entangled in this metaphor of the invisible hand. In the real estate business during the boom of the 1990s, greed was a prime motivator. Wealth was the goal, and many achieved it not only from real estate sales and investments but from computer technology as well. The overall economic consequence was known but overridden by short-term greed.

Subprime Mortgage Issues Relative to Race and Discrimination

Lander, Barker, Zabelina, and Williams's (2008) article, "Subprime Mortgage Trends: An International Issue," brings predatory lending and borrowing, mortgage fraud, unrelated mortgage brokers, off-balance sheet activity, and Asia into the conversation and takes these problems globally. The primary issue was that the recommendations these authors made could stabilize the problems but not without new government regulations and laws in order to achieve. African Americans in the United States were the main target of subprime mortgage fraud.

The secondary issue was huge amounts of capital invested by Asia, not only around the world but in the United States as well. Predatory lending and borrowing was worldwide, and we now know it will take worldwide cooperation to contain and/or find solutions that will be sustainable for all. The strengths were that this crisis has affected the world's financial markets, and this research proves that the world will need to work on this problem together in order to challenge it in the future. The weakness centers on regulations and laws around the globe that will undoubtedly be very difficult, if not possible. Greed and morals are evident throughout the article that extends around the world.

According to Laurie's (2008) article titled "An Investigation of the Time between Mortgage Default and Foreclosure," African American families are foreclosed on faster than others, which highlights my hypotheses in this literature review. The primary issue in this piece was the examination of discrimination by lenders based on race, leading to foreclosure. This article was written to show how neighborhood characteristics can be used to discriminate against black and minorities in the foreclosure. The secondary issue is relative to a telephone survey in New Orleans, Louisiana, from 1985 to 1990.

These results were used to determine the independent effects of race and neighbors' characteristics on to the extent of lender assistance during the foreclosure process. The strengths of this study were verifying deliberate discrimination on the part of lenders toward African Americans and their neighborhoods in homeownership in the United States of America. While no apparent weakness is present in this research, I think the connection between unemployment rates and income disparities has a direct effect on mass foreclosures in African American communities.

In the article by Howell (2006), "Exploring Race and Space: Concentrated Subprime Lending as Housing Discrimination," the primary issue was how African Americans get treated in financial issues relative to borrowing money on an existing loan or trying to purchase home not only by mortgage brokers but by banks and other lending institutions as well. This article was written to highlight problems with subprime lending and housing discrimination in African American families and communities in the United States. The locations of some examples in this article were south Chicago and Washington DC in 2006.

The secondary issue was that subprime lending was five times greater among black borrower, and most of them could have qualified for a prime loan; this would show that black people were cheated in financial issues relative to real estate transactions. Strengths of this article lie in the author relying on government policies and laws to explore these issues. Another is publishing this article in the California law review. He recognized subprime mortgage was a new way of discrimination against black and minorities living in communities that earlier were redlined by banks and federal programs. They now easily loan them money for homes but make serious profits in most cases. There were few weaknesses because this author was ahead of the bubble busting but knew it was coming. I think the author knew it would be an economic crisis eventually, but he did not know how severe it actually would be; we all know the results of these unethical and ill moral practices based not only on greed by lenders but on greed by Wall Street and other countries as well.

Immergluck and Smith (2006) argue in the article titled "The Impact of Single-Family Mortgage Foreclosure on Neighborhood Crime" that, as the primary issue in this article, the effects of foreclosures in African American neighborhoods do include increases in crime in those areas. For example, breaking in vacant houses for fixtures such as pipes, furnaces, hot water heaters, and bathroom parts like toilets and shower heads, and, if possible, the homeless will move in the property. This article was written to find out if foreclosures have additional effects on neighborhoods other than financial effects; the authors found that violent crimes were more significant than the type of crimes previously mentioned.

The secondary issue deals with regulations and policies relative to mortgage lending and the handling of high-risk subprime credit flow. Chicago's neighborhoods were mentioned in this piece because this area serves as an excellent example relative to subprime lending activities. The connection among race, homelessness, greed, and morals is very evident throughout this study. For example, race and homeless people are clearly variables in this piece. Greed and moral behavior explain why different policies and regulations in real estate mortgage lending are so vital to reconvert from this economic crisis we are struggling with in America and in other parts of the world as well.

McMurray and Thomson (2003) argues in "The Influence of Race in Residential Mortgage Closings, as their primary issue, that discrimination in the United States changed in form by subprime lending. Mortgage lending is directed to races of people living in depressed communities, netting lenders billions of dollars in profits during the real estate boom of the 1990s. This article was written to highlight how globalization of mortgages took place by bundling them as selling them as securities in global investment markets. The secondary issue showed lending money for housing to a group that had been previously denied the loan. The need and want were deeply embedded in these poor and low-income groups, and this translated into the making of billions by the greedy mortgage lenders and investors.

The strength of this article is that it really exposes what the real estate boom was all about, which was using race discrimination woes of both sides to make money. The weakness of that plan is that it caused a worldwide economic crisis. The opportunity now is to implement new polices and regulation to ensure this will never happen again and that all of us are treated fairly in housing issues in the future. A threat is that many want to continue to make money or do not want to treat people of color equally when it comes to housing sense. This is and always will be a serious sources of wealth. Real estate ownership is still the best way to stop living in poverty. A society needs the rich and the poor, and no one wants to be the latter.

According to Immergluck (2008), from "The Subprime to the Exotic; Excusive Mortgage Market Risk and Foreclosures," the reason this article was written was to analyze the recent trends in mortgage finance in order to recommend plans that would reduce the negative consequence of high-risk home lending for their own communities. The primary issue was that since the mid-1990s, mortgage market products in concentrated neighborhoods led to much of the foreclosure problems. This represented the subprime mortgage mess. Another important issue was that this led to influx of capital from Asia. Wall Street traders invented a way to package real estate mortgages and sold them on the stock exchange, which led to the current financial crisis.

The strength of this article was that the author recommends the rebuilding and restricting housing in these neighborhoods that need help. The weakening of the housing markers in concentrated foreclosure areas should be a wakeup call for mortgage lenders and policy makers that it is time to change these areas into new more profitable homes. The opportunity is real because regardless of past practices, the people living in these areas are human beings and always will need somewhere to live in. It is time to bring them off the fringes of this society into the main arena because it is the right thing to do in the twenty-first century.

Chapter 3: Methodology

This study will incorporate data from the National Association of Realtors, the Department of Housing and Urban Development (HUD), and from participatory observations based on the author's experiences as a real estate broker in Illinois by using a brief case study of his company. The methodology will be mixed. The main questions will be as follows:

- What will the future in real estate industry look like relative to the needs of African Americans for the rest of this century in the United States?
- How will the foreclosure problems be solved?
- If greed is the reason there are so many foreclosures today, then how and why do the morals of business professionals and government officials need to be examined?
- How do the foreclosure problems affect African Americans future?
- Why are African Americans families and communities more vulnerable?
- What will the future be like in homeownership for African American families in the United States?

These questions will be researched and analyzed in this book.

Orr discusses real estate mortgage foreclosures from all sides, using business and sociological perspectives. The author lives in Chicago and will visit the National Association of Realtors (NAR) library and research up-to-date information not only on foreclosures in these areas but other real estate issues as well. The author shows the past, present, and possible future in the real estate industry not only in the African American communities but in other places in the United States as well. The federal real estate laws today are being debated by Congress in order to find sustainable solutions to the many problems facing the industry. What is the connection of African American foreclosure issues to topics that follow and are used in this book?

The National Association of Realtors is the best source for any real estate issues; they are going on a bus tour starting in Chicago on March 5, 2011, talking to people about home ownership in the United States. Poor management and greed cause ineffective and unethical behavior in real estate transactions. Illinois Broker Management refers to current laws and regulations associated with managing real estate offices in the state of Illinois. Chicago, Illinois, foreclosure problems are seriously growing.

The US Conference of Mayors' (2010) survey of homelessness in various cities like Chicago, IL statistics on homeless families and individuals shows that most of these people are African American; the point here is that the numbers will grow larger because of foreclosure. This survey shows that the lack of affordable housing is the main reason for homelessness not only for individuals but for families as well. The main solutions mentioned in this report are more subsidized housing and more and better employment opportunities. Family cause of homelessness is poverty, and individual's causes include substance abusers. Foreclosures connects to people already living in poverty, and they do not have employment opportunities.

According to the US Census (2008), "Income, Poverty and Health Insurance in the United States," the question here is how does this report relate to foreclosure issues? Income is the main problem of African American s that prevents them from buying and keeping homes. After living in poverty for so long, paying bills in most cases is a new experience in many cases. Health insurance relates because of many living without proper methods of taking care of personal hygiene on a regular bases can cause illnesses, which can be dangerous to others in society. The statistics verify facts concerning living conditions relative to African Americans. How do bankruptcy laws help or hurt this foreclosure issue? This author thinks bankruptcy laws were bad for homeowners, but new regulations with mortgage loan modification rights may make it better.

This could give people a second chance at the American dream of homeownership. Bankruptcy can help clean up credit and debt issue. Housing sales are at its lowest levels in the entire country; for example, many real estate sales people are leaving the business and financial institutions hurting because loans are only being made to people with exceptional credit ratings.

The *Civil Rights Act of 1964*, the right to shelter, is part of the continued existence of all humanity.

> An act to enforce the constitutional right to vote, to confer jurisdiction upon district courts of the United States of America to provide relief against discrimination in public accommodations, to authorize the attorney general to institutes suits to protect constitutional rights in public facilities and public education, to extent the commission on civil rights, to prevent discrimination in federally assisted programs, to establish a commission on equal employment opportunity, and for other places.

Health is the most important thing to human beings, not only of your family but of others as well. A safe and clean living condition is absolutely essential for a healthy productive life. Unfortunately, too many African Americans are sick and suffering from mental problems. They also have untreated diseases because of none or unsanitary housing; all of this are already problems in America. Increases in the numbers of foreclosures can only make things worse . . . The Constitution of the United States is related to the foreclosure issue because of the human rights addressed in that document. The articles in this review relate to real estate mortgage foreclosure while looking at economics, politics, business, and sociology.

Does government intervention help or hurt the situation?

H1 If mortgage foreclosures keep increasing, then humankind's greed will keep increasing as well.

This signifies someone is going to benefit from this issue. The author thinks Wall Street and speculators are profiting the most. The reason why this is happening is not only greed but a deeply rooted lack of concern for the rest of society. Regulations by public officials will determine if foreclosures will decline.

H2 If African American poverty rates increase, then lack of morals by many in society will increase as well.

This acknowledges the United States as the richest country in the world. Also, the poverty rates are getting higher all the time, for which part of the blame goes squarely to government leadership. According to Obama (2004), "There is a moral deficit in the United States" and perhaps the world as well.

A good example is the lack of public officials to pass rules of law that would solve poverty problems. Redistribution of wealth in the country will determine if poverty can be a problem of the past in the twenty-first century.

H3 If low-income housing increases and becomes a regulated government policy, then unemployment rates will decrease.

This depends on rebuilding America to meet the future of the green economy and population growth by building any new single and multi-units to replace and increase the present supply in housing. This is because time is of the essence in fixing the infrastructure of America. This has been kicked down the road too many times already. This would create jobs and decrease the role of unemployment. The passage of the necessary laws by policy makers will determine future growth.

Research Question:
Does mortgage foreclosures and the plight of not only African Americans but other Americans to find and keep good affordable housing need more government intervention?

The regulation of the housing policy can build low-income housing all over America. The reason why this is a good time is because of the need to rebuild cities in the United States. Green homes and buildings are needed to help with future global warming. The ability of politicians to vote on policies and laws will determine the type of housing that will prevail in the future. The key questions in this study were as follows:

- How do foreclosure problems affect African Americans future?
- Why are African Americans families and communities more vulnerable?
- What will the future be like in homeownership for African American families in the United States?

In this study, the author tried to use several approaches such as qualitative, quantitative, participatory observation, a case study, secondary analysis, a comparative analysis, and a change process in order to highlight the foreclosure problems and add to the literature. The author gives some steps and strategies to help buyers and sellers of real estate, and some possible solutions on behalf of the African American community relative to foreclosures and real estate issues. He used 80 percent scholarly journal articles. The other sources were not only participatory observation, but research of government documents as well. Some data from a survey by the US Conference of Mayors 2010 will serve as part of statistics in order to show the facts of this huge problem. It will include variables such as race, income, greed, employment, morals, and other relative items. After creating a table using the survey cities used by the Conference of Mayors as a base, NCSS (2007) will be used to analyze the statistics.

The method is mixed in order to show aspects of questions that need to be answered and classes taken, which led to this type of inquiry. This study will be a secondary analysis, asking questions about the effects of mass foreclosures in cities; it does not cover all cities but should give us a general understanding of the problems of the homeless population. *A Greedy Society* will show the poor working and middle class hoping for the American dream being sadly disappointed in America. They have been lied to, cheated, and discriminated against; not only in housing but in employment opportunities as well. This is an investigation of the impact of mortgage foreclosures on African American families and communities in urban areas like Chicago, Illinois, in the United States. Much of the data are drawn from the American Conference of Mayors Survey Report 2010 on Hunger and Homelessness in this secondary analysis. The cities in this report will serve as part of the sample cities. Some survey questions are in the Appendices.

Table 1.

Survey of Cities

Location	Foreclosure	Unemployment	Population	Median Income	Poverty
Boston MA	1.8	8.7	613,411	51,688	18.7
Charleston, SC	1.3	10.4	113,234	48,259	20.3
Charlotte, NC	1.5	10.2	685,002	52,530	12
Chicago, IL	2.5	12.1	2,741,455	46,911	20.6
Cleveland, OH	2.9	12.2	408,101	26,701	30.5
Dallas, TX	1.5	8.3	1,227,082	40,796	22.6
Denver, CO	3.2	8.5	598,707	45,831	18.4
Detroit, MI	4.5	28.3	777,493	28,730	33.3
Des Moines IA	N/A	6.7	200,010	43,583	14.5
Gautama, NC	1.5	13.3	66,981	43,101	19.1
Kansas City, MO	1.6	11.9	436,402	45,824	16.4
Los Angeles, CA	2.9	12.4	3,803,383	48,882	19.4
Louisville, KY	0.8	10.7	566,861	44,254	16.1
Miami, FL	5.2	12.2	343,192	28,333	25.6
Minneapolis, MN	1.4	8.2	360,914	48,724	21.3
Nashville, TN	1.5	9.3	601,129	45,581	17.3
Norfolk, VA	1.0	9.3	234,220	40,416	18.9
Philadelphia, PA	1.0	10.3	1,447,395	36,976	24.1
Phoenix, AZ	6.0	9.5	1,252,257	50,140	18.9
Portland, OR	1.2	11.7	560,194	50,979	14.4
Providence, RI	1.5	14.9	171,128	38,426	25.4
Sacramental	5.2	13.9	452,849	50,958	16.1
St Paul, MN	1.4	9	268,962	45,831	18.4
Salt Lake UT	1.7	6.9	185,411	45,199	14.3
San Francisco	1.0	9.9	808,976	73,798	11
Seattle, WA	0.9	8.2	582,490	61,786	11.6
Trenton, NJ	N/A	12.5	83,092	35,397	22.5

Source: US Conference of Mayors Survey 2010.

Chapter 4: Findings

In the 1990s, real estate sales and refinancing soared in the United States. Greed and morals relative to real estate sales, refinancing, mortgages, and foreclosures are the variables that will be considered in this study. The effects of these problems relative to African American families and communities will be analyzed. The United States economy has experienced the worse downturns since the Great Depression of the 1930s. Real estate foreclosures are at the center of this problem. African American homeowners and communities have been affected the most because they were the target of the fraudulent practices by mortgage lenders trying to make profits. Real estate has always been a profession that had the potential of unethical practices, but this started getting out of hand during the 1990's boom. Well, in 2009, the bubble has busted and spilled its effects not only in the United States but around the world as well.

In order to observe this from a global perspective as well, the author will investigate real estate matters in several other countries briefly. These countries are Australia, United Kingdom, Ireland, Republic of China, Switzerland, Philippines, and South Africa. The main questions are as follows:

- How did we get in this mess in the first place?
- Why have greed and the lack of morals become an issue in all of this?
- What role does government policies play in all of this?
- What will determine if the world overcomes this economic downturn with a sustainable solution for the future?

Key Role Players in Real Estate

Accountants are used in all areas of the real estate industry; for example, a broker keeps escrow accounts and needs them to help keep books in order. Accountants also help brokers engaging in property management. Appraisers are the people who price the property's value. They are the reason high values on real estate have soared in recent years. They determine the price of each square foot of the building on each floor. Attorneys' roles are many, but the main function is providing buyers and sellers legal advice at closings, the reason being real estate documents are legal and confusing for the average individual.

Real estate brokers are responsible for all factors involved in the transaction from listing the property to closing the sale. For example, he/she or an agent lists a property. A buyer is found; this is where the other players get involved, but the broker is the manager of all activities. It is his/her job to close the sale with as few problems as possible and see that everyone gets paid what they are due from the transaction. Construction companies build new homes and buildings and use a broker to handle finding the buyer; however, the process is still managed by the real estate broker. There are many different players to act as counselors in real estate transactions, which depend on their particular expertise.

Government regulators is the key to controlling the way businesses treat consumers. The lack of enough or correct regulations in most aspects of business activity not only in the United States contributed greatly to the problems we face now. But other countries as well helped escalate these economic crises we find ourselves in today. This has been happening and building up for many years. A good example is that the mortgage brokers and mortgage lenders found a way to make plenty of money by refinancing existing loans above their actual value. The author will go into detail about regulations in the later chapters. Salespersons, insurance companies, and title companies have made plenty of money as well until the financial crisis that the world is struggling with now. The author's years of participatory observation has compelled him to write this book.

Table 2.

Unemployment rate (%) for July 11, 2011

African Americans	16.2
White Americans	8.1
Nationwide	9.1

Source: MSNBC News Report on that date listed above.
This is one reason for more foreclosures in African American communities. If jobs are not created quickly in the United States, then foreclosures increase in all areas. In December 2011, the nationwide unemployment has decreased to 8.6% and 2012 has been predicted to be even lower.

    This table represents unemployment rates that influence mortgage foreclosures because income for working-class Americans has not increased in at least a decade. If the income is not increasing and prices and/or account payables are still increasing, then the ability to pay will decrease.
    Wall Street in New York City is the financial district near the east river; it is the home of the stock exchange. New York City is the financial capital of the world, according to Litowitz (2005), "The Corporation as God," and Haywood and Wygal (2004), "Corporate Greed." They both agree that corporation power leads to admiration by many and leads them to unethical behavior that can also lead to crime. Many main street people feel cheated because of the huge incomes and bonuses given to executives and traders on Wall Street. Even Wall Street executives are afraid of living in poverty. They see images on television and on the streets; they may be greedy for that reason, making sure they never become poor.
    The Census (2009), American Community Survey, revealed relative to rental cost nationwide that 42.5 percent experienced cost that consumed 35 percent of renters' income or more. The highest amount of rent was in the metro area of Casper, Wyoming, and the lowest was in Pittsburg, Pennsylvania. The range for housing cost ranged from 23 percent to 64 percent. The point here is even if you live in the lowest area like Pittsburg, but is not working regularly, it will be hard to maintain shelter.
    The rates for men in the workforce decreased for ages sixteen to fifty-four from 2008 to 2009. Women experienced a slight increase, but men and women over fifty-five years of age stay about the same. These statistics show a trend

that affects African American families because they were already living in high-poverty areas nationwide. According to this survey, thirty-one states have increased in numbers and percentages of people living in poverty between 2008 and 2009; no state had a statistically significant decline in either the numbers or percentages during this period. These statistics tell the author he is correct with his concern about this group becoming a homeless race.

Morals are at the center of mortgage foreclosure because people need shelter to survive. The elements of right and wrong are the key to all of this because it is wrong to put humans out of their homes to live in the elements. This is what the homeless are dealing with. Religion is lacking any effective solution to the lack of morals in the world today as demonstrated by many at the top of the economic ladder in this society. The author thinks selfishness and the lack of morals within too many in societies will always cause problems among human beings.

Litowitz's (2005) article, titled "The Corporation as God," demonstrates the enormous power of multinational corporations around the world, many of which originated from the United States. They think they should not pay taxes and obey environmental laws if it disrupts their profit goals. In many countries, politicians regulate or deregulate to fit corporate profit goals. A corporation uses parts of profits to elect certain politicians in order to maintain their profit margins. The economy of many countries depends on the action of corporations operating in that country. For example, the oil companies such BP and Exxon Mobil and others have dependency that has reached epidemic proportions. In these cases, corporations are acting as gods because they are literally doing whatever they want to do, which is to make more money.

According to Haywood and Wygal (2004), "Corporate Greed vs. IMA's Ethics Code," the framework for ethical conduct, which included terms like competence, means performing duties according to relevant law, regulations, and technical standards. Confidentiality is keeping secrets that have a direct relationship to corporation business strategies. Integrity is a personal individual innate feeling dealing with doing right or wrong relative to being good or bad. This can be hard to do as a member of corporations that insist on maximizing their profits. Objectivity from the corporation perspective can be very different than the individual perspective. For example, some individuals might engage in an unethical or illegal activity in order to keep their job. Ethical behavior can be strained by corporate decisions relative to profits that satisfy shareholder, stakeholders, and others the corporations think they are representing at the expense of the consumer in most cases.

A good definition of crime according to Wellford's (1999) article titled "Crime" may be appropriate at this time in real estate matters in the United States. Crime has always presented a problem. Quoting Wellford (1999):

> If it is against criminal law, it is a crime. It is societies acting through their governments that make the rules declaring what acts are illegal. Hence, war is not a crime. Although it is the most violent of all human activities, it has not been declared illegal by governments or their agencies. But, petty theft—the stealing of a loaf of bread—is a crime because the laws of most states and nations have said so (p. 1).

The crimes committed in this piece were greed and a lack of morals by most of us around the world. One of my instructors said, "If you put an honest politician in office for two, four, or six years, handling all of our money, some of that money will stick to them when they leave office." This is an example of how it works in a society where your success depends on your bank account balance.

Religion plays a role in our lives because of the questions it raises about life, behavior, and death. Quoting:

> It has been said that thoughts of death lead necessarily to the development of religion. It is difficult to image what need there would be for religion in a world where no one ever died or became ill. All religions attempt to give answers to basic questions. From where did the world come? What is the meaning of human life? Why do people die and what happens afterward? Why is there evil? How should people behave? In the distant past these questions was answered in terms of mythology. Much of literature deals with them. Modern scientist investigates them (p.1).

The last two questions relate to the current economic crisis because selling real estate mortgages under false pretenses reflects evil and bad behavior on the part of Wall Street executives. I think gambling and greed played a major role in this economic crisis. This gambling and greed have not only spread among American stakeholders and investors but around the world as well.

Regulation is needed in practically all aspects of society. This includes laws by public officials of city, state, and federal government. The federal administration between 2000 and 2008 deregulated many aspects of business, which resulted in the real estate foreclosure problem. The new administration has been trying to change this situation. The American Recovery and Reinvestment Act of 2009 provided funding and assistance to several programs including the emergency food and shelter program, the emergency food assistance program, the neighborhood stabilization program, and the homeless prevention and rapid rehousing program, and problems of improving their quality of life in America. I think these programs are good, but the question remains whether they will help African Americans not become homeless in record numbers? This book is being written to highlight the problems of improving their quality of life in America.

Financing a home purchase for African American families has always been a daunting task in the United States. Discrimination is at the top of the list of factors that causes this problem for this group. Credit and debt issues are not to be overlooked as well. The subprime mortgage issues of the last decade canceled out redlining by banks and other lending institutions which includes not making loans to minorities and their neighborhoods because they started giving these loans at higher interest rates by adjustable rate mortgages, which consist of increasing monthly payments over a time period of one to three years, which can and do contribute to mortgage foreclosures. The African American people are dealing with many other problems such as gun violence and drug abuse. The problems of maintaining shelter make their quality of life in America very hard to improve.

Comparing and contracting the differences between real estate brokers and real estate salespersons begin with their roles in this mortgage foreclosure problem. The broker is not only the owner of the firm in most cases, but they are usually the manager as well. They are responsible for the day-to-day activity of the business. The salesperson usually functions as being self-employed under an agreed-upon contract with the broker. The broker is responsible for all of their actions in most cases. Relative to sells during the boom years, they both made a lot of profits. They both could have been guilty of unethical or illegal practices based on the evils of greed that have touched almost everyone in America. In the old days, brokers had more control of what salespeople/agents could do, but today with advanced uses of technology, that control diminished considerably. They can do many things without the broker ever knowing about it. Trust plays a major role in this type of agreement in today's business environment.

Chapter 5: Discussion and Conclusion

Orr thinks the economic crisis in the world will not begin to fully recover until the housing market makes a serious turnaround relative to values, and until the foreclosure problem is considerably slowed down not only in the United States but in the rest of the world as well. This mortgage foreclosure problem is not local, but global, in scope. Since 2006, home values have decreased by 33 percent in the United States. This trend will need to stop and reverse in order to begin to solve this problem. The politicians are debating job creation; there will not be any created until real estate property values stop decreasing. The economy was based on real property values. That was why they called homeownership the American dream. This economy is still the largest in the world at 14.6 trillion dollars; in order to maintain this in the future, we need to reinvent ourselves. Better education and innovation will be the key in doing this (Obama 2011).

According to Castaneda's (2004) dissertation, titled "Financial Literacy," teaching financial literacy in African American families and communities is critically needed so they can manage money and keep their homes. Learning when the race has been deprived of knowledge for so long will be a real challenge for many of them. They need to try harder to handle financial matters better. Staying on what is perceived as a low-paying job can pay off in the long run. The author started in a low-paying occupation sixteen years ago; he managed to make a good living by working overtime. There was plenty because the turnover rate in this occupation was very high. He understood the problem of being unemployed and cared enough about himself to tough it out, while others would just quit. Rohm (1993) said, "Keep trying until your skills change."

Litowitz's (2005) article demonstrates the enormous power of multinational corporations around the world, many of which originated from the United States. They think they should not pay taxes and obey environmental laws if it disrupts their profit goals. In many countries, politicians regulate or deregulate to fit corporate profit goals. A corporation uses parts of profits to elect certain politicians in order to maintain their profit margins. The economy of many countries depends on the action of corporations operating in that country. For example, the oil companies such as BP, Exxon Mobil, and other gas/oil companies have dependency that has reached epidemic proportions. In these cases, corporations are acting as gods because they are literally doing whatever they want to do, which is to make more money. Regulations and tax breaks are the key to their success.

Shlay's (2006) piece hit the heart of why this author wrote this book. The primary issue was policies dealing with low-income home ownership and all of the related variables. The secondary issue was the way this argument diverted policy maker's obligation to create policies for affordable housing. This piece was written to amplify how law makers in the United States avoid issues affecting the low-income or poor minority of the population in the United States of America. The setting was in any city or small town where the poor are in need of affordable housing. The policy in the housing industry was not to build affordable housing; rather, the policy was to sell high priced houses to low-income people.

According to Bond and Williams (2007), the primary issue was to show the lending to low-income and minority buyers. Starting in the 1990, this did not affect segregation in cities like Chicago. The secondary issue was deregulation of the mortgage lending industry transformed that business from redlining practicing of the past. Redlining means not lending to black or African American borrowers. The article was written to demonstrate this move in lending did not help the segregation of different groups in America. After decades of residential segregation and redlining, lending institutions started giving mortgages to black and minority borrowers though out the United States. The objective was to influence the real estate sales and profit margins. The data came from the Home Owners Disclosure Act of 1992 to 1999 and from the 1990 to 2000 Census Data.

In Bertrand, Mullainathan, and Shafer's (2006) piece, the primary issue was psychological perspective in decision making not only by the poor but by others as well. The reason this article was written was to demonstrate how the lack of monetary resources affects decision making by the poor. The issues that matter relative to implications for future policies are as follows:

- Simplicity for filling out forms and applying for benefits offer by government policy

- Persuasion relative to poor people's participation in programs that would help them
- Marketing government and non-profits are rare; perhaps, they should do more of this type of informing people.
- Program details could be better understood if marketed correctly.
- Honesty and accountability are very important in communicating to the poor by government agencies.

According to Clark (2009), the primary issue was that the current economic crisis was based on unbalanced lives where the economy was built on social injustice and greed. The reason this article was written from a Christian perspective was that the problems in this world has a direct relationship with human's relationship with a belief in a higher power (i.e., God). The secondary issue looks at income disparity and/or inequality not only in the United States but in the rest of the world as well. Barolo and Hochguertel's (2007) article was written to show there is not enough data on household liabilities in many countries, and that there is a need to look at consumer debt around the world. The primary issue was household debt including mortgages and other credit problems as well. The secondary issue was to make sure the data are correct and abundant throughout the world. The strength lies in the time of publishing this in 2007 because the real estate bubble burst in 2008.

According to Connery (2006), discrimination practices and the other problems in housing is monitored by the Department of Housing and Urban Development (HUD) in the United States. The primary issues in this piece compared fair housing laws in the United States and the United Kingdom relative to housing discrimination. The secondary issue includes their differences and what each can learn from these differences in fair housing laws. African American families have always had trouble with housing in the United States. Edmiston (2009) tells us about low-income foreclosure rates, which are where the crisis started because of subprime mortgages in these areas. The secondary issue was to show how over time the foreclosure crisis moved into higher-income areas between 2006 and 2009 and some reasons for this happening. The locations in this analysis were Wyoming, Colorado, Nebraska, and Florida.

According to Fuentes's (2009) article, the primary issue was the impact that predatory lending has played on poor and low-income people seeking the American dream. The purpose for writing this piece seems to be an attempt to get states like California to reform its lending laws relative to predatory and fraudulent practice in real estate sales and mortgage lending. The secondary issue focuses on greed and the lack of morals relative to people who cannot help themselves and who are too trusting in real estate matters.

Based on Statman's (2009) article, the primary issue was trying to find a balance between free trade and regulated markets. The secondary issue observed humans behavior toward one another relative to free trade. Discovering they will not treat each other fairly means a stronger regulation would protect us against ourselves and other people. It will force most of us to deal more fairly in business and financial matters. This article was written to show the free market believers that not only can one institution bring down others, but financial markets are built on confidence and trust.

In Landis and Mc Cluire (2010), there were three issue concerning housing investigated in this study: affordable housing, assist low-income renters, and enforced fair housing act in the United States. This article was written to evaluate and analyze trends in housing policies and organization administrating these policies in order to make them more effective. The method used was to revise the history of housing policies and programs to ascertain the effectiveness of these programs. They look at empirical studies as well. The results relative to recommendations were focused on low- and moderate-income families and to provide the funding to keep proven programs growing and make them easier to access and more transparent.

Holyoke (2004) was focused in the Washington DC area, investigating policies that require partnership with the federal and local governments and nonprofit community organization and social capital of individuals to solve the social problems of that community. The author's findings indicate this may work in some areas but not in areas such as poor African American communities. The primary issue in this article was to get problems solved by people in that community so the federal government could limit and reduce the assistance provided. The secondary issue was to push communities to take action on their own problems. This does not work in areas where poverty rates are high, because policies require them to act for their own interest. This author thinks this is why the problems in these areas are so bad.

According to Haywood and Wygal (2004), the framework for ethical conduct included terms like competence, which means performing duties according to relevance law, regulations, and technical standards. Confidentiality is keeping secrets that have a direct relationship to corporation business strategies. Integrity is a personal individual innate feeling dealing with doing right or wrong relative to being good or bad. This can be hard to do as a member of corporations that insist on maximizing their profits. Objectivity from the corporation perspective can be very different than individual perspective. For example, some individuals might engage in an unethical or illegal activity in order to keep their job. Ethical behavior can be strained by corporate decisions relative to profits that satisfy shareholder, stakeholders, and others the corporations think they are representing at the expense of the consumer in most cases.

Mazer and Ariely's (2006) article was written to show how dishonesty in day-to-day life is so high among too many of us. The primary issue and the secondary issue in this study are greed and morals. Greed and morals are the secondary issue not only in this study but in this author's research as well as he writes about foreclosures in America and the impact it is having on African American families. The strengths include looking at dishonest behavior in several ways: caused by external rewards, caused by internal reward mechanism, and caused by self-deception. From a psychological perspective, the authors use internal issues to change or prevent dishonest behavior in life.

The article by Howell (2006) shows how African Americans get treated in financial issues relative to borrowing money on an existing loan or trying to purchase home not only by mortgage brokers but by banks and other lending institutions as well. This article was written to highlight problems with subprime lending and housing discrimination in African American families and communities in the United States. The locations of some examples in this article were south Chicago and Washington DC in 2006.

For Immergluck and Smith (2006), the primary issue goes to another reason for writing this book. The effects of foreclosures in African American neighborhoods do include increases in crime in those areas. For example, breaking in vacant houses for the fixtures such as pipes, furnaces, hot water heaters, and bathroom parts like toilets and shower heads and, if possible, the homeless will move in the property. This article was written to find out if foreclosures have additional effects on neighborhoods other than financial effects; the authors found that violent crimes were more significant than the type of crimes previously mentioned.

McMurray and Thomson (2003) argue that discrimination in the United States changed in form by subprime lending. Mortgage lending directed to races of people living in depressed communities netted lenders billions of dollars in profits during the real estate boom of the 1990s. This article was written to highlight how globalization of mortgages took place by bundling them and selling them as securities in global investment markets. The secondary issue showed lending money for housing to a group that had been previously denied. The need and want was deeply embedded in these poor and low-income groups, and this translated into the making of billions by the greedy mortgage lenders and investors.

Immergluck's (2008) study was written to analyze the recent trends in mortgage finance in order to recommend plans that would reduce the negative consequence of high-risk home lending for their own communities. The primary issue was that since the mid-1990s, mortgage market products in concentrated neighborhoods led to much of the foreclosure problems. This represented the subprime mortgage mess. Another important issue was this led to influx of capital from Asia. Wall Street traders invented a way to package real estate mortgages and sold them on the stock exchange, which led to the current financial crisis.

The author would recommend that not only African Americans families focus on the following items relative to their quality of life issues with the main concern being housing and/or shelter but other Americans as well. Education is the most effective way to live a better life not only in cities like Chicago but also in other cities and states around the world. Success in life starts with being employed on a job that they can depend on.

Personal income for most Americans went down in the decade of 2000 to 2010 in the United States. Relative to housing and education policies, I found in Lipman (2008) that the mixed-income school and housing did not solve the problem of fair housing and education for minority groups such as African Americans. This mixed-income plan started in Chicago, Illinois. The point was to bring people living poverty households would have a chance to get better education. According to one of President Obama's speeches: "The best solution to poverty is a world class education." Saving by many Americans is very low relative to their future needs. I found that financial literacy is a need for many people not only African Americans, but they are the ones that has been held back relative to education and housing.

Orr thinks saving 10 to 30 percent of every dollar people earn will help in financial literacy and using credit correctly and avoiding unneeded debt. They have been highly abused by many because of consumer addiction in many cases. Determination and persistence are keys to being successful in life and getting an education, good housing, and decent credit. The elements of employment and income to pay bills have gone down in recent years. Changes in life are continuous and require the ability to adage by humankind not only in this society but the rest of the world as well. African Americans should forge alliances to bring about real change in all areas of their quality of life. This secondary research effort relative to housing and obtaining a better quality of life for the African American community will need vast expansion in the future in order to continue this debate for the good of all humankind. More study will be required to give justice and make the correct changes in their lives.

In today's world, selfishness and greed are phenomenal problems not only in the United States but around the world as well. Obama (2011) argues there is a moral deficit, and this has to change in order for the country to reach its full potential. For example, all stakeholders, meaning everyone in society, can be blamed for the financial problems; it is because everyone is obsessed with being rich and powerful people. This is not possible, so fighting over resources are the results. This has left the majority poor, and a few minority (20 percent) owns the wealth.

Money is the root of all evil, according to the Holy Bible (King James Version). Debt is a serious problem not only for individuals but for the US government as well. Sex has always been used to attract money and wealth from other humans around the world. Wealthy men and women are busy people in most cases and are used to buying stuff, so sex is just another item for many of them. Entertainment is important for them when they find time. Many Americans tend to want this type of life for themselves. This is selfishness, and greed comes back into focus. The point here is even poor people do not pay their bills and mortgage in some cases because of seeking entertainment

The younger generation learns moral behavior from their immediate surroundings, meaning home and parents. If there is no moral behavior exercised at home, then the young people will suffer. Older generations that came of age in the late 1940s have neglected their service to God in this society. Instead of worshiping the Almighty God, too many Americans are worshiping idol gods. For example, we admire music and rap artist, movie stars, football and basket ball players, and other famous people with plenty of money or a glamorous lifestyle. The legacy of African Americans is deeply embedded in poverty and the lack of enough resources; therefore, any opportunity to attain wealth is attractive to them in many cases.

Some people will not hesitate to use these vices, gambling, cheating, lying, and yes killing, to obtain wealth. Between 2005 and 2009, the wealth lost among African Americans was 53 percent, 66 percent for Hispanics, and only 16 percent for white Americans. This created a continuous wide gap relative to wealth between the races. The crime rates among these groups are disproportionally higher as well. When human beings are suffering and living on the fringes of society all of their lives, elements of right and wrong or good and evil would not enter their thought patterns in many cases. The problem of those who are doing well in society is they do not want to be like these people, so they engage in many unnecessary activities to obtain more and more, which is greed. Morality does not enter their thought pattern in many of these cases. The more millions of dollars they make, the more they want.

Change from the Bottom Up:
Kotter and Cohen (2002). *The Heart of Change:*
Why people succeed and why they fail at large-scale change

Kotter's Eight-Step Change Process:
1. Increase urgency: Raising a feeling of urgency so that people start telling each other "we must do something" about the problems and opportunities. Reducing the compliancy, fear, and anger that prevent changes from starting.
2. Build the guiding team: Helping pull together the right group of people with the right characteristics and sufficient power to drive the change effort. Helping them to behave with trust and emotional commitment to one another.
3. Get the vision right: Facilitating the movement beyond traditional analytical financial plans and budgets. Creating the right compelling vision to direct the effort. Helping the guiding team develop bold strategies for making bold visions a reality.
4. Communicate for buy-ins: sending clear credible messages about the direction of the change. Establishing genuine gut level buy-in that shows up in how people act. Using words, deeds, and new technologies to unclog communication channels and overcome confusion and distrust.
5. Empower action; removing barriers that block those who have genuinely embraced the vision and strategies. Taking away sufficient obstacles in their organizations and in their hearts. So they behave differently.
6. Create a short-term win: generating sufficient wins fast enough to diffuse cynicism, pessimism, and skepticism. Building momentum. Making sure successes are visible, unambiguous, and speak to what people are deeply concerned about.
7. Don't let up: helping people create waves and waves of changes until the vision is a reality. Not allowing urgency to sag. Not ducking the more difficult part of the transformation, especially the bigger emotional barriers. Eliminating needless work so you don't exhaust yourself along the way.

8. Make change stick: ensuring that people continue to act in new way despite the pull of tradition, by rooting behavior in reshaped organizational culture. Using the employee orientation process, the promotion process, and the power of emotion to enhance new group norms and shared values.

We see, we feel, and we change our feeling and thinking. There is a need for more than a few heroes in a turbulent world.

There is increase urgency in revising the real estate industry in the United States because it is the key to growth of the economy and create jobs. Orr thinks we should change the way real estate is purchased and sold. There should be three categories, high income, middle income, and low income pricing, of homes so everyone, regardless of financial position, can afford a home. Shelter is a universal right and necessity for all humankind for survival. In order to achieve this, we must build the guiding team from the bottom up. We must organized by identifying the need for people's survival in this life.

These people will attract policy makers and world leaders of governments to join the team and help get the vision right. We must communicate for buy-ins not only of America's leaders but of leaders from around the world as well. They must empower action for all of us to see that all people have good, clean, and sanitary shelter to protect us from the elements such as wind, rain, heat, and cold. We in the United States can solve this housing problem here. Perhaps we can become a model and create a short-term win. This long-term goal may take generations, but it can happen if we don't let up. We cannot start this process now; we need to make change stick into the future. We see the problem, we feel the need, and we change the way we look at providing shelter for the people (Kotter and Cohen 2002).

President Barack Obama's movement in America is a prime example of this type of change process. He argues that change comes from the bottom up, not from the top down. The idea comes from the top, but the people will need to act to implement that change. Many things need changing in this society. Cities like Cleveland, Ohio; Chicago, Illinois; and others are trying to find ways to prevent home prices and values from decline Massive foreclosed properties with little value are being demolished by city government, trying to stabilize home prices in certain neighborhoods. Chicago is planning to do the same along with other cities. Change does come from the people at the bottom of the economy when they become fed up with the situation or problems. Will government intervention help or hurt the situation? The people are the government, and the public officials they vote to lead are supposed to make laws that benefit the entire population, not just a few wealthy individuals or corporations.

Does mortgage foreclosures and the plight of not only African Americans but of other Americans to find and keep good affordable housing need more government intervention? Yes, but selfishness and greed in life and business have created an atmosphere of distrust not only of individuals but of policy makers as well. America is becoming more divisive than ever before. This may be irreversible relative to its future success. Real estate regulations is imperative to slave this economic crisis low income housing is must with sensible mortgage terms for new buyers that seek the American dream.

Lazy people are present in all occupations of work. In the last four decades, Americans have become extremely lazy and seem to want someone else to work for them. This will not be sustainable for this society to continue being a world leader. After these economic crises or after the real estate bubble busted, unemployment in all areas has reached epidemic proportions. Many people will do many things to get along until they are again working low-paying jobs they had never dreamed they would need to do. Many people worry about paying taxes, but taxes are what make the economy work if used properly by the government. When you are not working, taxes stop; taxes start again once you are working again.

The families foreclosed on will need to rent shelter. Rentals today are as much or more than mortgage payments without any benefits. Buyers of homes enjoy many benefits if they keep up with payments long enough. Investors make their money buying low in resalable areas and selling them higher for profit and/or rent property until sold. The American Jobs Act proposed by the Obama Administration on September 9, 2011, should help slow real estate mortgage foreclosures. They will refinance homes that are in risk of foreclosure at a low rate of interest. Hopefully, this act becomes law and addresses these real estate mortgage foreclosures. The author has tried to write this as contemporary as possible; however, this mortgage foreclosure problem is still in progress and may be decades in its resolution especially in the African American communities.

The New York stock exchange or Wall Street's participation in the mortgage foreclosure issues has a direct relationship to people with retirement accounts such as 401k or 403b. Some public officials would like to do the same with Social Security benefits as well. They are playing the market like investors and corporations. Gambling with your retirement funds is not good. Greed is a serious problem around the world because all of us want to ensure or improve our quality of life. Morals are not in abundance in this world because many of us do not fear God, but fear death.

President Obama's administration is working on new policies to affect the mortgage foreclosure problem that is harming the entire economy. These problems started during the administration of Reagan in the 1980s. The change that needs to be made is to stop trickle-down economics and implement a system that will put the people first and a policy that will help people at the bottom instead of all the wealth going to the top. Generations in the future need this type of change for the United States to maintain its leadership in the world. Younger children born between 2000 and 2010 will come of age in 2020; they will need homes to live in America. Orr is not a preacher but used the foundation of the Ten Commandments while thinking with his head and his heart to write about the problems of America today. Information is closer to what he is trying to accomplish here not only for African American people but the rest of us as well. The hope of a more diverse society is one of the goals he seeks to achieve with this book.

What is the real estate industry's role in the economy? Homeownership is not only the backbone of this economy but creates many jobs when a home is built, leased, or sold as well. Current foreclosure statistics according to the US Conference of Mayors 2010 shows that many cities have implemented programs that hopefully will prevent homelessness after foreclosures. Most people that were evicted because of foreclosure still have resources; people living with them would be displaced into full homelessness.

Gambling by Wall Street and some individuals is not the cure to America's financial problems; it seems to me the cause of our problems. Some of the Republicans in the US Congress and others would like foreclosures to continue to bottom out and investors buy cheap, fit them up, and rent out until the market gets better then they sell them for profits. Mortgage companies have really tightened down on the qualifications needed to buy a home in today's market. Fannie Mae and Freddie Mac help people with 90 percent of all mortgages in the United States. Many public officials would like to get rid of these government agencies because they are backed by the government. The large banks are holding on to billions of dollars, which have a serious effect on the job market in this country. Retirement is based on three pillars: pensions, bank savings, and Social Security benefits. Wall Street is gambling with the first two and wants the last piece—Social Security. This would not be good for the poor or middle class in America. The president of the United States has ordered new policies relative to homeowners refinancing their mortgages in an effort to save their homes from foreclosures. This situation is manmade and should not have occurred in the wealthiest country on earth.

We don't know where this country will wind up on the other side of this financial crisis. One side of a divided country wants to give up on democracy for more money for only a few. The other side wants to continue down the path set up by the constitution for a more perfect union. Accounts that are payable in excess of fourteen trillion dollars for the United States debt has caused many policymakers to panic and resort to austerity measures such as cutting all the social programs that define democratic society. This is not good because the economy cannot rebuild itself unless people have jobs and spend money.

The real unemployment rate is about 17 percent among African Americans and 9 percent for all Americans. Multinational corporations based in the United States create jobs overseas, which diminish jobs in this country to increase their profits. The labor cost and tax burden is where they benefit from using this strategy. These methods have a direct relationship to Occupy Wall Street Movement in cities all over the United States. The economic crisis was manmade and continues because of political stalemate in the US Congress. Taking austerity measures is the only way of solving their debt problems. The lack of action in building up the economy and creating jobs reminded this author of the fall of the Roman Empire's political, economic, military, and other institutional failure along with invasions from outsiders. Other theories called the fall a transformation brought about by changes.

Social unrest in the United States may cause a transformation that will not be the same again for this country. The Tea Party under the Republican Party and the Occupy Wall Sheet has the position of changing America as we know it forever. The right and wrong of each different group are critical to the future of the country relative to falling or just transformation. African Americans are rooting for Occupy Wall Street to transform the distribution of wealth. This would make it better for employment and finding and keeping shelter. Orr thinks the real estate industry will recover, and we will as a country come out to find after this recession is over. The majority of Americans want this country to continue as the greatest nation in the free world.

President Obama's Helping Families Save Their Homes Act—with recent adjustments—should be the place to start rebuilding the housing market. Real estate has to play a major role in recovery from this recession.

> For what is a man profited, if he shall gain the whole world, and lose his own soul? Or what shall a man give in exchange for his soul?
>
> King James Version, Holy Bible, New Testament, Matthew 16:26

And again I say unto you, it is easier for a camel to go through the eye of a needle, than for a rich man to enter into the kingdom of God.

> King James Version, Holy Bible,
> New Testament, Matthew 19:24.

These quotes are directed to those folks that aspire to be wealthy. Those folks that gamble away their income to the point of losing their homes need to change this behavior. And those folks that are the top wealthiest individuals in the country that are so greedy they avoid paying their fare share of income taxes that would help the less fortunate. Further research is required because this economic crisis and real estate mortgage foreclosures will be a problem for well into the future. Kotter's eight-step change process should be continuous and repeated many times to keep the process going. The survey question in the appendices should be answered and returned to this author, if possible, by readers of this book that can relate to them.

References

Barolo, G. & Hochguertel, S. (2007). Household debt and credit: economic issues and data problems. Economic Notes, 36, 2, 115–146.

Bertrand, M., Mullainathan, S.,& Shafir, E. (2006). Behavior economics and marking in aid of decision making among the poor. Journal of Public Policy and Marketing, 25, (1), 8–23.

Bond, C., & Williams, R. (2007). Residential segregation and the transformation of home

Bowman, J. B. & Williams, R. L. (1997). Ethics in Government: from a winter of dispirit to a Spring of hope. Public Administration Review, 57, 6, 517–526.

Castaneda, R. (2004). *Financial Literacy*. Argosy University Chicago.

Clark, C M. A. (2009). A Christian perspective of the current economic crisis. The American Economist, 53, 1, 16–29.

Ciulla, J. B. (2003). The Ethics of Leadership. Thomson Wadsworth.

Connerly, C. E. (2006). Fair housing in the US and UK. Housing Studies, 21, 3, 343–360.

DeNavas-Walt, C., Procter, B. D. & Smith, J. C., U. S. Census Bureau, Current Population Report (2008). Income, Poverty and Health Insurance Coverage in the United States, 60 236.

Durant, W. & Durant, A. (1968). *The Lessons of History.* Simon & Schuster, New York.

Edmiston, K. D. (2009). Characteristics of high-foreclosure neighborhoods in the tenth district. Federal Reserve Bank of Kamas City, Economic Review, 51–77.

Ferguson, A. & King, T. C. (2006). Taking up our elders burden as our own: NWSA Journal, 18, 2, 148–169.

Franklin, A. J. & Franklin, N. B. (2000). Invisible syndrome: a critical model of the effects of racism on African American males. American Journal of Orthopsychiatry, 70, 1, 33–41.

Fuentes, N. L. (2009). Defaulting the American Dream: Predatory lending in Latino Communities reform of California's lending laws. California Law Review, 97, 1279–1335.

Goodchild, B. (2003). Implementing the right to housing in France: strengthening or fragmenting the welfare state? Housing Theory and Society, 20, 2, 86–97.

Gotham, K. F. (2005). Tourism gentrification: The case of New Orleans Vieux Carre (French Quarter). Urban Studies, 42, 7, 1099–1121.

Greenspan, A. (2006). Discussion board posters debate scope of industry regulations. National Mortgage News, 12.

Guynn, J. (2005).Ethical challenges in a market economy. Do the right thing when nobody is looking. Vital speeches of the day, 71, 13, 386–391.

Haywood & Wygal (2004). Corporate Greed vs. IMA'S Ethics Code. Strategic Finance, 45–50.

Hartman, E. M. (2006). Can we teach character? An Aristotelian Answer. Academy of Management Learning and Education, 5, 1, 68–81.

Holtoke, T. T. (2004). Community mobilization and credit: the impact of nonprofits and social capital on community reinvestment act lending. Social Science Quarterly, 85, 1, 187–207.

Howell, B. (2006). Exploring race and space: concentrated subprime lending as housing discrimination. California Law Review, 94:10, 101–150.

Immergluck, D. & Smith, G. (2006). The impact of single-family mortgage foreclosure on neighborhood crime. Housing Studies, 21, 6, 851–866.

Immergluck, D. (2008). From the Subprime to the Exotic; Excessive mortgage market risk and foreclosures. Journal of American Planning Association, 74, 1, 59–76.

Keep, W. (2003). Adam Smith's imperfect invisible hand. Business Ethics: A European Review, 12, 4, 343–353.

Kotter, J. F. & Cohen, D. S. (2002). *The Heart of Change:* Harvard Business School Press, Boston, MA.

Krummeck, S. (2000). The role of ethics in fraud prevention: a partition's perspective, Copyright of Business Ethics, 9, 4, 268–272.

Lander, G. H. Barker, K. Zabelina, M. & Williams, T. A. (2008). Subprime mortgage trends: an international issue. International Atlantic Economic Society, 29, 1–17.

Landis, J. D. & Mc Cluire, K. (2010). Rethinking federal housing policy. Journal of the American Planning Association, 76, 3, 319–350.

Lauria, P. (2008). An investigation of the time between mortgage default and foreclosure. Housing Studies, 19, 4, 581–600.

Leshinsky, R. (2008). Knowing the social in urban planning law-decision making. Urban Policy and Research, 26, 4, 415–427.

Lipman, P. (2008). Mixed-income schools and housing advancing the neoliberal urban agenda. Journal of Education Policy, 23, 2, 119–124.

Litowitz, D. (2005). The corporation as god? Journal of Corporate Law. 501–538.

Litzky, B. E., Eddleston, K. A. & Kidder, D. (2004).The good, the bad, and the misguided: how managers inadvertently encourage deviant behaviors. Academy of Management Perspectives, 91–103.

McMurray, J. P. & Thomson, T. A. (2003). The influence of race in residential mortgage closings. The Journal of Real Estate Research, 25, 4, 543–558.

Mazar, N. & Ariely, D. (2006). Dishonesty in everyday life and its policy implications. American Marketing Association, 25, 1, 117–126.

NCSS Statistical Software (2007).NCSS Software from www.ncss.com

Newman, K. & Wyly, E. K. (2004). Geographies of mortgage segmentation: the case of Essex County, New Jersey. Housing Studies, 53, 1, 63–83.

Obama, B. H. (2004). *The Obesity of Hope* Three River's Press.

Orr, C. H. (2005). *Homelessness: A Challenge to African American Males*. Tate Publishing. Oklahoma

Orr, C. H. (2009). *A Night Watchman* Xlibris Publishing, Indiana

Salkind, N. J. (2000). *Statistics for people who think they hate statistics*. Sage Publishing Inc.

Sassen, S. (2000). *Cities in a World Economy* Pine Forest Press.

Sekaran, U. (2003). *Research Methods for Business: A skill building approach*. John Wiley & Sons Inc.

.Shlay, A. B. (2006). Low-income homeownership: American dream or delusion: Urban Studies, 43, 3, 511–531.

Squires, G. D. & Kubrin, C. E. (2005). Privilege places: race, uneven development, and the geography of opportunity in urban America. Urbn Studies, 42, 1, 47–68.

Statman, M. (2009). Regulating financial markets: protecting us from ourselves and others. Financial Analysts Journal, 1–10.

The National Association of Realtors (2011). Michigan Avenue. Chicago, Illinois.

Trimiew, D. M., & Greene, M. (1997). How we got over: the moral teaching of the African American church on business ethics, Business Ethics Quarterly, 7, 2, 133–147.

U. S. Conference of Mayors (2010) Status Report on Hunger & Homelessness. This report presents the results of a survey of the twenty-seven cities that comprise the U.S. Conference of Mayors' Task Force on Hunger and Homelessness. Respondents were asked to provide information on emergency food assistance and homeless services provided between October 1, 2009, and September 30, 2010.

Wight, J. B. (2007). The treatment of smith's invisible hand. Journal of economic education, 341–358.

Appendices

A.
Survey of Doctorate Classes Completed
Classes: Doctorate of Business Administration, DBA

Classes Incorporated in this Book:
Managing Change
Contemporary Problems and Issues in Education
Introduction to the Dissertation Process
Advance Statistics Methods
Business Research Methods
Global Management Models
Survey Techniques
Advance Human Resource Management
Business Policy Seminar
Ethics in Business and Management
Organizational Development and Change
Corporate Social Responsibility
Management Science
Stress Management Control
Organizational Behavior
This is the order of Doctorate business classes taken at Argosy University/ Chicago DBA program participated in by the author from Sept. 2004 to Jan. 2008.

This table represents the author's credibility for writing this book.

B.
Survey Questions
1. Are African American communities affected more than others relative to foreclosures?
   Yes
   No
   Maybe
   Not sure

2. Did greed play a role in foreclosure problem?
   Yes
   No
   Maybe
   Not sure

3. Does the lack of correct regulations by the government have a role?
   Yes
   No
   Maybe
   Not sure

4. Can America solve this ethical dilemma in the real estate profession?
   Yes
   No
   Maybe
   Not sure

5. Do loan modifications help the overall future of real estate issues?
   Yes
   No
   Maybe
   Not sure

6. What type of market for sales is there in your location?
   Excellent
   Good
   Fair
   Poor
   Remarks:

7. How well is your production?
    Excellent
    Good
    Fair
    Poor
    Remarks:

8. How well is your company's production?
    Excellent
    Good
    Fair
    Poor
    Remarks:

9. How is the job market in your town?
    Excellent
    Good
    Fair
    Poor
    Remarks:

10. How does the future of real estate sales look in your area?
    Excellent
    Good
    Fair
    Poor
    Remarks:

11. African Americans are worse off than the other groups because of foreclosure problems?
    Agree
    Strongly agree
    Disagree
    Strongly disagree
    Remarks:

12. The real estate industry will come back in the future?
    Agree
    Strongly agree

Disagree
Strongly disagree
Remarks:

13. The government will regulate the industry and make it better than before?
Agree
Strongly agree
Disagree
Strongly disagree
Remarks:

14. The overall job market will get better soon?
Agree
Strongly agree
Disagree
Strongly disagree
Remarks:

15. The economic situation in the United States was caused by all of us?
Agree
Strongly agree
Disagree
Strongly disagree
Remarks:

The results or responses to these questions were not enough to incorporate in this book; nevertheless, please respond and send me a copy of your responses if possible.

Table 3

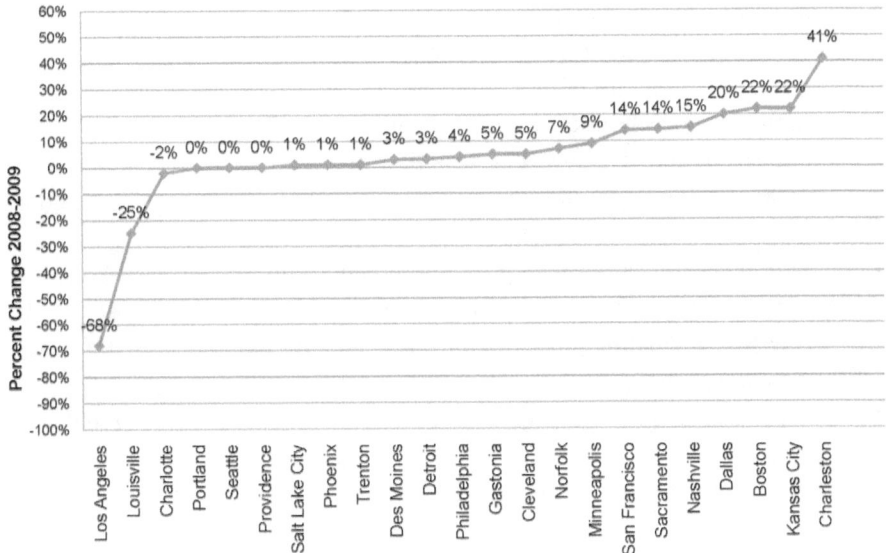

From the US Conference of Mayors Survey, 2009

Changes in family homelessness are significant in this book because African American families have been the victim of man's inhumanity to man for as long as they have been in America.

C.
Survey of Change Process:
Change from the bottom up.
Kotter & Cohen (2002). *The Heart of Change:*
Why people succeed and why they fail at large-scale change

Kotter's Eight-Step Change Process
- Increase urgency. Raise a feeling of urgency so that people start telling each other "we must do something" about the problems and opportunities. Reduce the compliancy, fear, and anger that prevent changes from starting.
- Build the guiding team. Help pull together the right group of people with the right characteristics and sufficient power to drive the change effort. Help them to behave with trust and emotional commitment to one another.
- Get the vision right. Facilitate the movement beyond traditional analytical financial plans and budgets. Create the right compelling vision to direct

the effort. Help the guiding team develop bold strategies for making bold visions a reality.
- Communicate for buy-ins. Send clear credible messages about the direction of the change. Establish genuine gut-level buy-in that shows up in how people act. Use words, deeds, and new technologies to unclog communication channels and overcome confusion and distrust.
- Empower action. Remove barriers that block those who have genuinely embraced the vision and strategies. Take away sufficient obstacles in their organizations and in their hearts so they behave differently.
- Create a short-term win. Generate sufficient wins fast enough to diffuse cynicism, pessimism, and skepticism. Build momentum. Make sure successes are visible, unambiguous, and speak to what people are deeply concerned about.
- Don't let up. Help people create waves and waves of changes until the vision is a reality. Do not allow urgency to sag. Do not duck the more difficult part of the transformation, especially the bigger emotional barriers. Eliminate needless work so you don't exhaust yourself along the way.
- Make change stick. Ensure that people continue to act in new ways despite the pull of tradition, by rooting behavior in reshaped organizational culture. Use the employee orientation process, the promotion process, and the power of emotion to enhance new group norms and shared values.

We see, we feel, and we change our feeling and thinking. There is a need for more than a few heroes in a turbulent world.

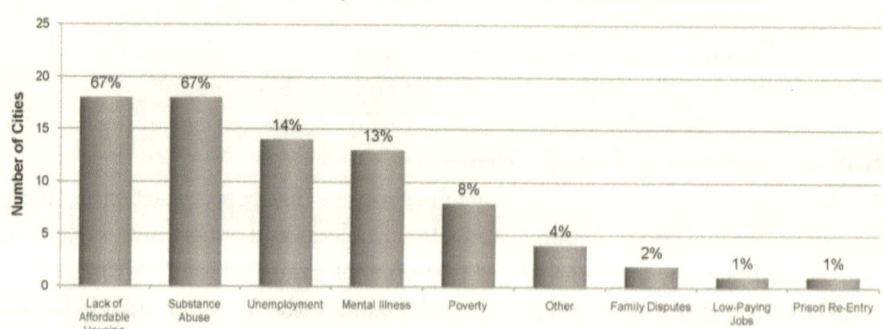

Exhibit 8. Top Three Causes of Individual Homelessness

From the US Conference of Mayors Survey, 2009

Lack of affordable housing and unemployment has a direct relationship to mortgage foreclosures and increases substance abuse (Orr 2005).

Resume

Charles Henry Orr

Summary
In 1998, I returned to college in order to improve my reading, writing, speaking, and computer skills. I've accomplished these goals, which are evident by the degrees I have obtained and the books I have published: *Homelessness* (2005), *A Night Watchman* (2009), and this book titled *A Greedy Society* (2011). All three books were done while working full time as a security officer in the Chicago-land area. I also have the credentials to be a private security contractor and private investigator in Illinois. Over the span of thirty-two years, I have engaged in and held a license as a real estate broker, not only in Illinois but also in the state of Ohio. I am well prepared, determined, and persistent enough to be an asset in any organization because I am a deliberate reader and researcher by design.

Education
ARGOSY UNVERSITY, Chicago, Illinois
DBA Doctorate of Business Administration/Management with all necessary classes completed, 2007
DEPAUL UNIVERSITY, Chicago, Illinois
MA: Sociology, 2004
BA: School for New Learning, Computer Technology and Real Estate Brokerage, 2001
THE UNIVERSITY OF AKRON, Akron, Ohio
AA degrees: Business Management Technology and Real Estate Brokerage, 1982

Work Experience
DePaul University 1 East Jackson Boulevard, Chicago, Illinois (2008–present)
- As a public safety officer, I am responsible for protecting and monitoring for unsafe or criminal activity that would harm anyone in my work area at the Loop Campus.

Burns International Security 6200 South Western Avenue Chicago, Illinois (2005–2008)
- As a security officer, I am responsible for monitoring all vehicles and checking identification badges at a trucking and railroad yard in Bedford Park, Illinois.

Barton Protective Services—Chicago, Illinois
Assistant Account Manager/Supervisor (2000–2005)
- Develop and implement security plans for a commercial office building with thirty floors.
- Supervise a staff of four security officers.
- Interact with diverse groups of people.
- Organize and prioritize tasks in a logical order to ensure timely completion.

The John Buck Company (1998–2000)
20 S. Clark Street in Chicago Loop, Security Officer
- Sign visitors in and out.
- Monitor and greet tenants.

American Protective Services (1996–1998)
- 515 N. State Street in Chicago Loop, Security Officer with the same type of duties listed above.

Before 1996, I was employed at The Press of Ohio, Alliance Realty, General Tire and Rubber Company, United States Gypsum Company.

License: Real estate broker, private detective, private contract security, and certified criminal defense investigator in Illinois.

www.ingramcontent.com/pod-product-compliance
Lightning Source LLC
Chambersburg PA
CBHW021009180526
45163CB00005B/1939